it's not me,
it's you

it's not me, it's you

the ultimate BREAK UP book

Anna Jane Grossman

and Flint Wainess

Da Capo

LIFE
LONG

A Member of the Perseus Books Group

Text design by Jane Raese
Set in 12-point Mrs Eaves

First Da Capo Press edition 2006

Library of Congress Cataloging-in-Publication Data

Grossman, Anna Jane.
    It's not me, it's you : the ultimate breakup book / Anna Jane Grossman and
Flint Wainess. — 1st Da Capo Press ed.
        p. cm.
    ISBN-13: 978-0-7382-1051-3 (hardcover : alk. paper)
    ISBN-10: 0-7382-1051-X (hardcover : alk. paper) 1. Separation
(Psychology)—Humor. 2. Man-woman relationships—Humor. I. Wainess,
Flint. II. Title.

PN6231.S495G76 2006
306.8902'07—dc22   2005032729

ISBN-13: 978-0-7382-1075-9 (U.K.)
ISBN-10: 0-7382-1075-7 (U.K.)

Cataloging-in-Publication data for this book
is available from the British Library.

Perseus Books UK
69-70 Temple Chambers
3-7 Temple Avenue
London EC4Y 0HP

Da Capo Press books are available at special discounts for
bulk purchases in the U.S. by corporations, institutions, and
other organizations. For more information, please contact the
Special Markets Department at the Perseus Books Group,
11 Cambridge Center, Cambridge, MA 02142,
or call (800) 255-1514 or (617) 252-5298,
or e-mail special.markets@perseusbooks.com.

1 2 3 4 5 6 7 8 9—09 08 07 06

To our exes: See what you drove us to?

Contents

Breaking Down the Breakup Book

INTRODUCTION

PART ONE

Getting Ready for Good-bye
(a.k.a. the Relationship)

Contents

PART TWO

The Breakup

PART THREE

Get Over It

Contents

EPILOGUE

Introduction

A Note from Flint and Anna Jane

Dear John and Jane,

We're sorry to have to say this, but we've decided to leave you. That's all we wanted to say.

Actually, wait. There's more. There's a lot more. Some of it is going to be painful, some of it is going to be funny, and some of it is going to make you want to check into a mental institution, but we promise, we're not doing this for us; we're doing it for you.

You see, it's not that we don't love you. Obviously, we don't love you, but that's not the point. The point is, we need to end things so that we can both move on with our lives. We should have seen from the beginning that it couldn't work with you, because you're the kind who falls in love hard and then wakes up one day to find that your lover had never really fallen at all. You're the one who fears being alone so much that you pinball from open arms to open arms.

Oh, uh, never mind—you're the one from the bar, right? The one that looked so good after sixteen beers . . .

No? Not you either?

Then you must be the one that we broke up with months ago but continues to believe that we can be "just friends," or the one who's just never really been into the idea of "monogamy," or the one who always falls for jerks, or the one who is starting to wonder if maybe you'd just be better off alone, or gay, or alone and gay.

More likely, you're the one that's just like all the others: you're the one who hates breaking up. You avoid it like the plague, because it's stressful and uncomfortable and, sometimes, downright scary.

Thing is—and sweetie, we know this is going to be hard to hear—you're going to have to get used to it, because most relationships just don't last. Those butterflies you feel during the first kiss? They're just moths dressed up in pretty clothes.

We're not only talking about marriages. We're talking about everything from hookups to decades-old civil unions to plain old boyfriend/girlfriend-ships. Hell, we're even talking about the Beatles and the cast of *Friends;* everyone breaks up eventually.

And most of us will spend high school, college, our twenties, and even our thirties breaking up more than we do just about anything else.

However, when we look for advice for the brokenhearted (and we've looked like Indiana Jones looking for the Holy Grail), very little of it rings true. *Everything happens for a reason,* they say. *It's important to get closure,* they say. *A clean break is best.*

Bullocks.

We say: they don't always happen for a reason, it's sometimes more important to get a new lover than it is to get closure, and, clean breaks don't exist, unless you didn't care all that much in the first place. Indeed, breakups are a dirty, dirty business, and it's time someone rolled around in the dirt. Breaking up properly, like synchronized swimming, is an art form, and getting over a breakup, well, that can be a lifelong endeavor.

Yet, for some reason, the things you do after a breakup—the uncontrollable crying, the self-loathing, the endless whining to friends—are considered shameful. And we think that's a shame.

So we decided to write a love letter to the breakup.

See, one of us recently turned thirty and has lost approximately seventy-five weekends to weddings in the past two years. He's tired of choosing between chicken and fish, and he's tired of having to give up Saturday, Sunday, and sometimes Monday in order to pretend to celebrate the union of Mr. and Mrs. Boring, who, chances are, will be sick of each other by their first anniversary. Tragically, he has now reached an age where he is getting invitations to second weddings.

Meanwhile, the other one of us—the more attractive one—has made a career out of writing about other people's nuptial bliss. She's documented the weddings of nearly a thousand supposedly happy, devoted couples for magazines and newspapers in the form of wedding announcements. She knows diamonds better than De Beers yet has never gotten one (sniff!). When she started to feel a little thrill of excitement every time she heard that a couple she'd written about got divorced, she considered finding a new career.

Don't get us wrong—we both think weddings are swell. Free drinks, free cake, old people dancing. Did we mention free hair spray in the bathrooms?

Problem is, no matter how many weddings we attend, we continue to feel like outsiders, like aliens who have arrived on earth to find a strange and perplexing mating ritual. That's because *our* love lives have always led to dead ends; we're better at understanding what happens when relationships don't lead to happily ever after.

However, we haven't stopped attending weddings entirely—in fact, it was a wedding that brought us together in the first place. We were, of course, the only dateless guests, so we had no choice but to talk. We could have cut out early and screwed, but that would've been rude, like throwing a wedding on a Sunday night or having a cash bar. Besides, we weren't sure we liked each other that much. Instead, we camped out at the martini station (near the fondue!) and began trying to outdo each other with tales of our own recent breakups.

Then, somewhere between the horrah and the hokey pokey, it hit us: entire industries have sprung up to support the betrothed, but while the future happy couples are getting all the love (and the gifts and the press and the sex), those of us who are breaking up are getting *bupkes,* other than some clichéd advice.

Where's our party? Where are our presents? Why don't we get to go to Aruba?

Struggling with these issues, we did what any other healthy American would do: we started a Web site.

On BreakupNews.com, we began chronicling the breakups of couples all over the world in the format of wedding announcements. With every broken heart's submission, it became clearer to us that the current breakup clichés weren't sufficient to explain a culture obsessed with getting out of it and getting over it. The stories people shared with us were so rich and hilarious and filled with life that we knew breakups weren't the p.s., they were the letter. So, we decided to combine some of what we've learned in our own lives with some of what we've learned from couples who have written us to create a practical guide to the breakup. How to do it, how not to do it, when to do it, where to do it, whether to do it, and what to do after you've done it.

After a discussion of the rich history of the breakup (cavemen did it, dinosaurs did it, French royalty did it, so why not you?), we'll take a magnifying glass to relationships and examine why so many of them fail. Then we'll help you "get ready for good-bye." In other words, we'll explain how to think about breakups preemptively—no, we never did this when we were dating you, honey, we swear. But, if we had, we would have weighed the worth of muddling through a bad relationship against the pain of just ending things. We would have mapped out the signs that a rupture is imminent, and then we would have done our best to make sure that you wouldn't be getting over us too quickly.

The next part of the book deals with the actual act of splitting up. You may need goggles for this section; it gets a bit nasty. Here you will learn how to break up like your favorite celebrity, as well as the proper breakup methods for every type of relationship. We'll also supply you with a lost-in-translation chart for what men and women really mean when they're breaking up with you, and a breakup glossary to help develop your heartbreak vocabulary. We'll even give you some suggestions on writing a breakup letter.

Last comes a section that we think you're going to like. It's all about the aftermath—the process of getting over someone. Obviously, getting over two people as magnificently handsome and talented as us won't be easy, but we think this section will help. You'll learn, among other things, what truisms about breaking up are false and what lies actually have merit, how to recognize the various stages of grief, and how to satiate any curiosity you might have about your ex by becoming an expert "Web stalker." If you've ever visited Rock Bottom, this is the travel guide for you!

Each section of the book also includes questions and answers to all your breakup-related questions, as well as survey results from our poll of five hundred losers like yourself.

Don't worry, sweets. We may be leaving you forever, but the next time you start a relationship (years and years and a lot of therapy from now), you'll be much better equipped for the inevitable split.

And by then, we hope you'll have really absorbed the most important not-so-secret secret about getting over a breakup: it will hurt like hell for a long time, and then one day when you think you'll never be able to survive another moment without us, you'll find yourself under someone new . . . and better.

Breakups are often treated like a memory box or a crazy aunt that should be locked in the attic. But we think that even though they can be ugly, breakups are something to be embraced, like Blossom. After all, they're unavoidable, and potentially a lot more interesting than another white wedding.

So, that's what our book is about. We hope you're cool with that. We've been brainstorming titles. We were thinking about maybe, "It's Not You, It's Me." But then we realized: that's never really the case. It's you. It's always been you.

We wish you all the best,

Flint and Anna Jane

P.S.: We're taking the cats.

A Brief History of Modern Heartbreak:
A Rich Past of Pain

I hate divorce.

—THE LORD (MAL. 2:16)

At this point in history, humans ought to be breakup experts—after all, it's something we've been doing for long enough. Exactly how long? It's a point that wise men have debated. "Divorce probably dates from the same time as marriage," according to Voltaire's estimate. "I think, though, that marriage is a few weeks older."

One keyhole into early breakup history is the Bible, supposedly a moral guide for us all. The good book is filled with romantic betrayal on almost every page—Delilah tortured Samson; Abraham kicked Hagar to the curb after she had his baby; even wise King David couldn't keep it in his pants when he saw the lovely (but very married)

Bathsheba slipping into the tub. According to myth, Adam had a first wife, Lilith, but she dumped him after he insisted on making her lie underneath him like a dead seal during lovemaking.

If, as scientists have learned, we produce a surplus of natural feel-good agents like serotonin and dopamine in our brains when we're in love, then it's logical that we'd get cranky with each other when the buzz inevitably wears off. Meanwhile, anthropologists have theorized that we're hardwired to stay in relationships only as long as it takes to create a child who doesn't need constant attention.

But before you blame humans for our unstable mating practices, consider that only 5 percent of mammals are monogamous. Birds will dedicate years to luring in a mate with all sorts of fancy songs and dances, only to dump their conquest once the deed is done. Even penguins, one of the few species to mate for life, have a breakup rate of more than 10 percent.

If King David and the penguins can't make love work, how can we?

Wherever there are men and women, or men and men, or hot penguin-on-penguin action, there will be heartbreak.

However, while there have always been breakups, the role played by romantic ruptures in our culture has changed dramatically through history.

Once upon a time, finding happiness and finding a mate were not necessarily tandem endeavors. Women in particular didn't have the luxury of being able to search endlessly for Mr. Right, let alone hop from sack to sack with Mr. Right Now. They were usually married—and were

---

BREAKUP CUSTOMS

Japan: Enter the *Wakaresaseya*

Why ruin your own relationship when you can hire a firm to do it for you?

The Japanese have taken breaking up to a whole new level, with the proliferation of *wakaresaseya*, loosely translated as "the breaker upper" or "separator." These relationship-termination specialists will literally break up for you, or they'll ruin your relationship to the point that your lover breaks up with you. According to Mark Magnier in the *Los Angeles Times, wakaresaseya* professionals are trained to play whatever roles necessary—CEO or flight attendant or prostitute—in order to prove that someone is unfaithful, or to lure someone into a situation that will lead them to want to break up with the person who has hired the *wakaresaseya*. In a society where women are often too polite to break off a relationship and risk alienating friends, it's a business that is soaring. They boast a nearly 100 percent success rate.

Hiroshi Ito runs one of the more successful firms, and has lured numerous young women into dalliances. He tells the *Christian Science Monitor* that "his work is 'not very virtuous.'" The women he tricks, however, generally don't develop deep feelings for him. "'But if they do, well, it's just a job.'"

---

often married off—in order to form a utilitarian pair, and to propagate the species.

Relationships were, for the most part, simple unions of practicality. Man and woman each served a purpose. Hunter, gatherer; father, mother; breadwinner, bread spender.

These forged unions weren't always joyous ones, but that was beside the point.

In much of the Western canon, great love was equated not with great happiness but with great tragedy—insanity, maiming, or premature death (think Romeo and Juliet or Anna Karenina). Romances that met an untimely end were depicted mostly as catastrophic moments that defined lives—events that led people to start wars or throw themselves under trains—or they were once-in-a-lifetime moments of incomparable personal sorrow.

Sure, there have always been courtesans and playboys and loose women, but heartbreak and dissatisfaction usually weren't the stuff of regular table talk, and rarely were reason enough to divorce.

So how did we enter this stage of history where almost everyone has experienced at least one earth-shattering heartbreak—and a smattering of smaller ones—by their junior year of high school? How did our lives become like romantic comedies, in which we are endlessly thinking and brooding and obsessing about the one(s) that got away?

First, consider that people live a lot longer than they once did, making "till death do us part" a lot harder to commit to—today, that might mean putting up with someone until they're, like, really, really old.

Add to an increased life expectancy the fact that, in the past century, life has gotten a lot easier for those of us who choose to remain single (or those of us who don't want to be single but can't get a second date). In a postagrarian world, dinner can be speared at the A&P, women can earn executive salaries, wash can be done by machine, and televisions can raise children. All this has made coupling more a matter of emotion than necessity—at least in the early premortgage stages of a union—and emotion is a lot less stable than dependence.

But nothing revolutionized our breakup culture like the sexual revolution—a moment in time that literally gave life to a lot of us. In the sixties and seventies, birth control allowed couples to love and leave each other without having to spawn, and education and new employment opportunities opened up to women. All this meant that many women who might have thought they had to get married just in order to survive in previous times now had more choices. With ladies no longer requiring men for stability, sustenance, and social acceptance, they could spend their lives loving and leaving guys as they wanted, in pursuit of prosperity or passion or just a good roll in the hay.

The media reflected these changes, shifting its focus from having most couples stay together—*The Honeymooners*—to having single people fend for themselves.

The more pop culture fed us with stories about love falling apart, the more we realized that it was okay to shed unsatisfactory relationships in the hopes of finding something better.

Dick Van Dyke Show? Nah. *Mary Tyler Moore Show*? Yeah!

Sam Malone, the Fonz, Carrie Bradshaw, Blanche Devereaux, Jerry Seinfeld—we let these beloved inveterate TV daters into our living rooms because we, like them, have become obsessed with finding true love, or at least a make-out partner.

In short, we were born into an era where settling down is no longer necessarily de rigueur. In this new world order, we don't stop looking around until we find the yin that

THE QUICKIE BREAKUP STAT PACK

Oh, you're in a relationship. Aren't you special?
No. You're doomed. Here's why.

→ In 2003, half as many people got divorced as got married.
→ 11 percent of murder victims in the United States are killed by a spouse or lover.
→ 43 percent of first marriages end in separation or divorce within fifteen years.
→ Divorce costs Americans an estimated $30 billion a year.
→ The average woman marries for the first time at 25.3 and divorces for the first time at 29. The average man marries for the first time at 26.9 and divorces at 30.5.
→ The state with the highest divorce rate is also the state known for quickie marriages: Nevada.
→ One out of ten Americans has been divorced.
→ Linda Chandler of Indiana has been divorced more than any other person: twenty-two times.

perfectly matches our yang, even if we don't really know what a yang is. With choosiness comes rejection; if finding Mr. or Mrs. (or Ms.) Right means stepping on some Wrongs along the way, so be it.

Of course, we all know couples who tried to buck this breakup culture. They shake their heads at your sad dating stories. They pretend to be there for you for like a week after you get dumped, but then they stop returning your calls. You hate them because you think they are happier than you when, most of the time, they're not. Most of them are as secretly jealous of you as you are of them. While they're arguing over who will take out the trash, you're at a bar, picking up someone trashy.

Healthy, happy coupling is made nearly impossible by a society obsessed with a fantastical vision of monogamy, the idea that you deserve to be loved like Buttercup in *The Princess Bride:* overwhelmingly, outlandishly, unconditionally. If your lover hasn't brought you a bouquet of roses by the second date, he's "not that into you" and you should move on. Of course, if he has brought you a bouquet of roses on the second date, then he is too into you, and it's creepy. Either way, you lose. We live in a culture that both inundates us with images of oozing sexuality and preaches that monogamy is the only truth.

Wasn't it better the way it used to be, when you just picked someone and suffered through until death did you part?

We don't think so.

We continue striving for new and better loves because, for perhaps the first time in history, we can, and because there's something about the breakup that can be as romantic as the coming together.

As hokey as it sounds, a world full of heartbreak is actually a world full of hope. Every time a romantic door closes, another one opens—at least that's what we tell ourselves.

A Timeline of Divorce, Heartbreak, and Infidelity

*Ah, yes, "divorce," from the Latin word meaning
to rip out a man's genitals through his wallet.*
—ROBIN WILLIAMS

4000 BC—Adam and Eve see each other naked. They try to just be friends, but it doesn't work out.

3000 BC—Animal-hide condom is invented in Egypt, making breakup sex a lot less risky.

2500 BC—Noah ushers animal couples onto his ark to save them from the Flood; any animal not in a committed relationship gets washed away.

1700 BC—In Babylon, Hammurabi—the Mr. Big of his day—states in his code that a man is allowed to leave his woman, but if they have kids she has to keep them.

1674 BC—Greek god Zeus, king of heaven, marries his sister Hera, but immediately regrets this choice and starts screwing around with gods and mortals alike. She tries to get revenge by holding him captive in Olympus, but it doesn't work, and he punishes her by hanging her from the sky by her wrists. Of course, Zeus gets all the press while the lovely and loyal Hera gets nothing but rope burn.

1200 BC—Menelaus launches the Trojan War after his wife, Helen of Troy, runs off with a dude named Paris.

1179 BC—Odysseus leaves his wife, Penelope, for seven years while he goes around sleeping with other women, all the while claiming he's trying to return to her. First utterance of the phrase, "Why don't you ever call me anymore?"

51 BC—Cleopatra and Antony have the first ever long-distance romance. It doesn't go so well. He falls on his sword, and then she lets herself be bitten by a deadly snake. They leave behind a gaggle of emotionally disturbed children to be raised by his ex.

18 BC—In Rome, the emperor Augustus passes a law permitting a man to kill any other man he finds screwing his wife in his own home.

270—Valentine, a priest in Rome, is killed when he decides to marry young couples against Emperor Claudius II's orders—Claudius wants young men to stay single because he feels they'd make better soldiers. The young men are cool with this, but the young women complain. Two hundred years later, in his honor, the pope officially makes February 14 a day to be feared.

331—Emperor Constantine I forbids Roman women from seeking divorce except when their husbands are proven to be murderers, sorcerers, or tomb raiders.

826—Pope Eugenius says divorce can be granted in cases of adultery, and the nonadulterer can then remarry. The adulterer, however, cannot get remarried, but can continue screwing other people's spouses.

900—In China, the Tang dynasty points the way to no-fault divorce, encouraging unhappy couples to separate peacefully and happily. Divorce agreements read as such: "Since we cannot live together harmoniously, we had better separate. I hope that after the divorce, you will be as young and beautiful as before, and may you find a more satisfactory mate. I hope that the divorce will not plant hatred between us in the future."

1492—Columbus stumbles upon America, leading to the first occurrence in this hemisphere of both STDs and pants.

1533—Henry VIII, king of England, marries his longtime lover Anne Boleyn after years of trying to get the Roman Catholic Church to grant him a divorce from his first wife, Catherine of Aragon. When the clergy won't let him legally rid himself of wife number one, he splits with the pope and makes himself head of a new church, the Church of England. Of course, he ends up executing his new wife three years later. Despite being fat and reportedly impotent, he goes on to kill and divorce his way through another four marriages.

1564—The Council of Trent officially sets down the canon law forbidding divorce among Catholics.

1583—In his writing on the Commandments, Gervase Babington, the bishop of Warwick, becomes the first person on record to use the English word *heartbreak*. He uses it in reference to the daily grief experienced among people who are married.

1762—First instance of a woman paying palimony. Catherine the Great of Russia kills off her doltish hubby, Peter III, and takes the throne for herself. During her thirty-four-year reign, she takes many lovers, often letting her ladies-in-waiting test-drive the young stallions to make sure they're up to the task of pleasuring her. When a romance falls apart, she sends the men packing with large chunks of cash, or else she just gives them their own country to run.

1820—King George IV of England tries to divorce his wife, Caroline, when he takes the throne and attempts to pass a bill to deprive her of the title of queen. The matter is brought to the courts, but the British public sides with Caroline, who revels in the attention, and a divorce is never granted.

1844—First rubber condoms appear on the market. Also first year that rubber condom breaks at a really inopportune moment.

1847—First mass-produced Valentine's Day cards become available in the United States. Also the first year when not receiving one from a lover could be given as a reason to break up.

1857—England passes a divorce law making it easier for common people to divorce—previously, divorces could be granted only by Parliament and were extremely difficult and expensive to obtain.

1900—Never a country to be outdone, the United States takes the worldwide lead in divorce by the turn of the century. By 1910, Canada cites America's soaring divorce rate as an example of the country's absence of social restraint; in that year, there are four times as many divorces in the United States than in Belgium, Holland, Switzerland, Norway, England, Scotland, France, Denmark, and Sweden combined.

1937—Ireland makes divorce illegal under all circumstances, despite the fact that 80 percent of its couples got married after seven beers.

1948—Alfred Kinsey's *Sexual Behavior in the Human Male* shocks America with its revelation that 50 percent of men have been unfaithful to their wives. Who knew it was so low?

1960—The Food and Drug Administration approves the first birth control pill, ushering in an era when it's suddenly a lot easier to separate the act of sex from the idea of commitment.

1969—California becomes the first state in the United States to permit no-fault divorces—divorces where neither party needs to accuse the other one of something awful in order to officially split.

1978—England welcomes the birth of the first "test-tube" baby, suggesting that there may be no greater need behind heterosexual copulation other than the desire of men and women to torture each other.

1980—Ronald Reagan becomes the only elected president in the United States to have gone through a divorce, and the only one to have gotten second billing to a monkey. His first wife was actress Jane Wyman; his second, Nancy Davis, was three months preggers when they wed.

1984—Motorola starts selling the first cell phone—the two-pound DynaTAC 8000X. The cost, $4,000, is nothing compared to the price paid by those who quickly discover the ease with which they can now dial their ex while drunk. In Wisconsin, Ida and Simon Stern become the oldest couple in the world to get divorced. He's ninety-seven; she's ninety-one.

1992—Vice President Dan Quayle holds up Murphy Brown as an example of poor "family values" in America, because the sitcom character has chosen to raise her child as a single woman (and teach future generations the accurate spelling of the word *potato*).

1995—Ireland legalizes divorce after 50.28 percent of the voting population announce they're in favor of it.

1996—Prince Charles and Princess Diana announce their intention to divorce after nearly fifteen years of marriage; the media seem thrilled, since it's clear Diana is a ten and Charles is like a four at best. After her death Charles waits a tactful nine years before marrying his longtime mistress, Camilla Parker Bowles, also a divorcée and a fellow four.

1997—Louisiana gives couples the option to have a "covenant" marriage, whereby they agree to waive their right to a no-fault divorce—they can divorce only in cases of abuse, adultery, or abandonment.

1998—The first lady stands by her man after President Bill Clinton gets caught with his pants down in the Oval Office, and the evidence is preserved on a blue dress from the Gap. Bob Dole gets an erection again after doctors start prescribing Viagra, giving older men more incentive than ever before to leave their wives for younger women.

2004—President George W. Bush tries to pass a constitutional amendment to ban gay marriage.

2005—Everyone who is anyone in Hollywood decides to do some dumping—Brad and Jen, Paris and Paris, Renée and Kenny, Jamie-Lynn, Tori, Jude and Sienna, Mischa, Denise and Charlie—making this the most important breakup year since, like, 2004.

))))— **My Worst Breakup** ——▶

by JT LeRoy

He was a Hollywood up-and-coming dude that was terrified of being outed, even though I wore a dress and very red lipstick most of the time we rendezvoused in our secret locale. Last time was at Hotel Vitale, a waterfront hotel in San Francisco ($699/night, his series got renewed). I've slumbered under the Bay Bridge, but never on it, and this dang close to it . . . 180-degree views of the San Francisco Bay.

I loathe getting naked in front of anyone, just the vulnerability of it, and I have scar and trust issues, but then I never had a bath butler draw a bath for me in a two-person limestone soaking tub! So I didn't insist the place was pitch black, as usual. It was like one of them TV seduction scenes with scented candles and rose petals. That goes a long way in compensating for flaws of the flesh, I reasoned. He said he wanted it perfect. For me.

We snuggled into the walk-in rain shower with floor-to-ceiling glass partitions—we made out on either side of the glass. After: order room service, he said; no worries about the expense. So I did, and then I lounged in an overstuffed bathrobe in bed and was fed by my hot stud. Alaskan Halibut Carpaccio with Jicama, Green Grapes & Pimeton de la Vera ($13), Whole Petaluma Chicken "al mattone" for two with Fennel, Almonds & Braised Greens ($49), and Hazelnut and Chocolate Zuccoto ($10) with a bottle of Perrier Jouet

"Fleur de Champagne" ($155). We watched a DVD of *Deadwood* (season one) on the suite's LCD flat-screen television.

The next morning, just as in a soap opera, he had vanished. He'd left me a note on hotel stationery on his side of the bed. He had supplied me a detailed total of all the expenses of our night—even the bath oil was named and priced. The rose petals had apparently cost $15.99. Underneath he'd written in a childish scrawl, "You are priceless to me, but this is my noble effort toward the infinity of your value. Alas, I can not afford you in this maddening Hollywood game I find myself now in. Please treasure our evening. My agent and publicist seized a huge ass chunk and my residuals have not kicked in yet so I will be paying this off for a very long time, always thinking of you. Please don't be bitter.

"There are chocolates, very dark like your love, under the pillow. They cost $36.97. Nothing of your worth. I will miss you. . . ."

I dragged out the chocolates, made fast work of them, then appropriated every fucking thing not nailed down in Room #816. Sheets, bedding, soap dish, all superlative quality. I signed the bill with little hearts and chocolate smeared fingerprints.

JT LeRoy is the author of *Sarah* and *The Heart Is Deceitful above All Things,* as well as the novellas *Harold's End* and *Labour.* He is also the editor of *Da Capo Best Music Writing 2005.*

PART ONE

Getting Ready for Good-bye
(a.k.a. the Relationship)

A relationship, I think, is like a shark, you know?

It has to constantly move forward or it dies.

And I think what we got on our hands

is a dead shark.

—ALVY SINGER, *ANNIE HALL*

It's not easy being a single person in a couples' world. You can't buy a single bed, because they're too small, yet a queen-size bed leaves you wondering what to do with that other pillowcase that comes with the set. Your toothbrush holder taunts you with its extra space. Even the car serves as a reminder that your passenger seat, like your life, is empty. Food won't do away with this bereft feeling either; you can't go to your favorite restaurant because there are no tables for one (sushi bars being a generous exception). And, while having sex with yourself is safer than doing it with someone else, it's just not quite as satisfying.

It's enough to make you want to . . . be in a relationship.

So, you couple.

And that is where your problems begin, because relationships are hard. Like, Rubik's Cube hard. They require communication and patience and gifts. Worse, they require dinner with your lover's family, or your boyfriend's female "friend" who doesn't talk except to tell you how she graduated from the same college as your lover, with the same degree, and they find the same jokes funny and have the same sign and—are they playing footsie under the table? Yes, relationships are ridiculously hard. In fact, most of the time, they end up being too hard. Yet, some of the time, you're so desperate not to be single again that you find you're clinging to a dead shark.

Eventually, however, you return to the Sisyphean cycle of the breakup.

Indeed, although this is a book about breakups, not relationships, the breakup can't exist without the relationship. We wish it could, but it can't. That's why we've taken a

PROFILES IN NOT-A-LOT-OF-COURAGE

The Ladies Gabor

The three Gabor sisters have had a cumulative twenty marriages among them and have been divorced nearly as many times.

Eva married five times and Magda married six, but Zsa Zsa took first place in this sibling rivalry.

Her first spouse was a Turkish diplomat. She was seventeen, and he was more than twice her age. She then went on to wed hotelier Conrad Hilton, who would later become the great-grandfather of Nicky and Paris Hilton, and was also briefly Elizabeth Taylor's father-in-law (see page 105). He fathered the one Gabor offspring. "Conrad Hilton was very generous to me in the divorce settlement. He gave me five thousand Gideon Bibles," she said. Rounding out her collection of husbands were, among others, oil magnate Joshua Cosden Jr. and Michael O'Hara, who, conveniently, was a divorce lawyer. She also married—and subsequently divorced—actor George Sanders, who would go on to marry and divorce her sister Magda before then killing himself. Now, Zsa Zsa—the only of the sisters who is still alive—is married to Frederic von Anhalt, and therefore bears the title "princess of Anhalt."

In the 1980s, she was given a polygraph test on a TV show and was asked if she made a habit of marrying for money. The polygraph wasn't able to decipher the veracity of her answer. But she was quoted as saying, "Getting divorced just because you don't love a man is almost as silly as getting married just because you do."

few precious pages to examine the anatomy of a relationship—how you can spot the different types that exist, why they sour, whether you can drink your way through the dog days, and why most of them will fail.

If you're seeing someone (and we'd really advise against it), you might want to start examining your own relationship as soon as possible. We're here to help point out the flaws in this thing you call a love affair.

Are we doing it because we're lonely and bitter? Yes. But we were also pretty lonely and bitter in our relationships, so it's more than that. In order to become an expert breaker-upper, you must first master the thing that you're going to break up with, that is, the relationship.

This is our guide to "getting ready for good-bye," to realizing that it's our happiness that counts. So if someone else is impinging on it, they need to go.

Do You Know This Couple?
Common Types of Relationships
and Why They Won't Last

I know happy couples . . .
but I think they lie to each other.
—JESSE, *BEFORE SUNRISE*

Like snowflakes or bad dates, no two couples are exactly alike. However, when closely scrutinized at barbecues and brises, patterns arise among them. For those who are post—first date but prebreakup identifying which kind of union you are in can help prepare you for its inevitable termination, or at least help you make fun of your friends. Here are a few of the more common breeds.

The "Mad About Yous"

How to Spot Them
Early on in their union, Mad About Yous are not shy about publicly displaying their mutual affection, even in places that are kind of gross, like the subway and the supermarket. Usually, MAYs are either very stable, self-realized people who truly believe they've found their ideal mate and are ecstatic about it, or seriously unstable and jump from one emotion-filled union to another, in pursuit of more endorphins, a bigger bathroom, and better air-conditioning. The unstable MAYs, however, believe they fall into the "stable" category.

The Best-Case Scenario
After raising Bobby, Cindy, Jan, Marcia, Peter, and Greg, the MAYs grow old together. They play a lot of tennis and go on cruises. They have sex, every day. They are generally hated by all of their friends at the club. Eventually, one of the members of this couple might reveal he or she is gay, but homosexuality cannot destroy the loving bonds that have been formed over the years, and the couple will still embrace warmly at televised family reunions.

The Worst-Case (and Significantly More Likely) Scenario
The passion that launched the relationship cannot be sustained, and a bitter and protracted breakup ensues. Once your idealized love has fallen from its pedestal, there is little hope the same joy will ever be experienced again. Both parties will probably require medication and a Costco-size box of Kleenex.

The "Bio Clockers"

How to Spot Them
Tick tick, tick tick. Although they may have been more tentative in previous relationships, Bio Clockers use the words *my boyfriend* or *my girlfriend* in every conversation once they meet one another, even if they've been dating for, like, a weekend. They might have shirked the idea of true love, but they've accepted that you can't always settle down with the person who makes your heart do the polka. They treat love more like a game of musical chairs. When you hit a certain age, the music stops, and you procreate with whoever is in the closest chair. In other words, they are passionate about . . . buying furniture together. They marry fast, and knock out a couple little ones faster.

The Best-Case Scenario
It's a relationship built on common values and mutual respect for what the other person brings to the union (for example, sperm or eggs). *Values* and *respect* are, in fact, words oft repeated in the household (which will give the relationship an uncanny resemblance to a Mafia movie). They're words that make the children want to gag, but they create a foundation for a happy home. Or, at least, happyish. There isn't a lot of passion or sex, but this makes it less awkward when the kids knock on the door wanting to sleep with mommy and daddy in the middle of the night because of the boogeyman. Toward late middle age, they will find new ways of channeling their passions. He will buy a sports car; she will join a knitting group; the kids will go to therapy. In short, happily ever after will be achieved.

The Worst-Case (and Significantly More Likely) Scenario

Once Junior can walk and talk, neither bio clocker is sure what's left in the relationship for them. The bio clockers start asking themselves some very serious questions. What was I thinking? Is this really the person with whom it was wisest to share my DNA? When's the last time we've gone to the theater, or the opera, or an underground cockfight? Isn't the kid now old enough to go back and forth between homes every other weekend? Sometimes, like in an arranged marriage, the couples grow to put up with one another . . . kind of like the cowriters of this book. But, just as often, they harbor secret dreams of strangling each other in their sleep (Flint is asthmatic; he'll go quick). But strangling is no solution. Seriously, we can't emphasize this enough: do not strangle.

The "Hooker Uppers"

How to Spot Them

They laugh uproariously at each other's stories, because they have not heard them before. They often punctuate bouts of Public Displays of Affection with moments of extreme awkwardness. They call their friends with revelations they've yet to digest ("Who knew he was a nose picker?!"). He doesn't know whether she takes milk in coffee, she doesn't know his middle name . . . but they both know that they prefer missionary to doggy style.

The Best-Case Scenario

The sexual chemistry remains, and the intellectual and emotional chemistry blossoms. The more they get to know each other outside the Bar Marmont, the more they enjoy each other's company. Eventually, they move in together and hook up seven nights a week.

The Worst-Case (and Significantly More Likely) Scenario

One member realizes that it's not healthy to start a relationship wearing beer goggles, and decides that a second encounter should be avoided—especially when the first e-mail from the other member contains four misspelled words and five emoticons. Nevertheless, the inferior speller insists on referring to the other member as his or her significant other. An uncomfortable breakup e-mail will take care of the whole thing, and the two will then avoid each other at parties forever after.

The "Make Your Parents Happies"

How to Spot Them

Their relationship is based on meeting the family at the club, or talking about upcoming events, or planning their wedding. They're the couple that work on paper but don't look all that enthused together in real life.

The Best-Case Scenario

They make each other's parents happy, and eventually make peace with the fact that they aren't spending their lives with their soul mates. In fact, much of their time

THE LADDER THEORY OF RELATIONSHIPS

According to writer Dallas Lynn's "Ladder Theory" (www.laddertheory.com), both men and women rank all potential mates on an imaginary ladder, or ladders. Men have one ladder. Near the top of the ladder, they put women they'd actively like to have sex with—women who might in fact be out of their league but whom they nevertheless aspire to bang. In the middle of the ladder are women whom men would have sex with when drunk, and at the bottom of the ladder are women whom men would have sex with when drunk but not admit it to their friends. For men, the meaning of life is to move up the ladder. So, if a man is dating someone on rung eight but then meets someone on rung nine, he is going to dump the eight and reach for the nine.

Women, meanwhile, have two ladders, their "real ladder" and a "friend ladder." Often, a man on the friend ladder isn't aware he's not on the "real" ladder, because, of course, he's put the woman on his real ladder. Attempting to jump ladders is extremely dangerous and almost never succeeds.

For women, the meaning of life isn't just to move up the ladder. They use one ladder to find the best possible friends, and the other to find the greatest lover.

According to this theory, a woman will place a man on one of the ladders mostly because of his attractiveness and her hypothesis about how much money or power he has, while a man uses looks as the major criterion. The rest of his judgment regarding her placement on the ladder has to do with how likely he thinks she is to put out quickly.

The conclusion to be drawn from the ladder theory is that the odds of any relationship working are very small. This is because the odds of two people meeting and placing each other on the same rung of their "real" ladder at the same time are slim.

together is spent scoffing at people who believe in "soul mates" at all. Okay, this is hitting a little close to home. We have to go cry now.

The Worst-Case (and Significantly More Likely) Scenario
They begin to resent both their parents and each other, and this eventually leads to adultery or, worse, really stupid hobbies like model airplanes or origami.

The "Buck Fuddies" (a.k.a. "Samantha Joneses")

How to Spot Them
They spend most of their time behind closed doors and are thus hard to spot. When they come up for air, they may be seen panting, pawing, or dry humping.

Typically, one Buck Fuddy calls the other when horny late at night, and then a night of sex follows. (NB: The sex these couples experience isn't always good, and is often worse than they'll admit.) If they run into one another when each is with someone else, the looks of discomfort are priceless.

The Best-Case Scenario
Thousands of happy orgasms are experienced. The sounds of lovemaking can be heard around the world. Buck Fuddies each use the promise of regular nookie to buoy themselves as they look for a more heartfelt, meaningful relationship. It gives them ballast and quells the need to jump into something so-so just to fulfill a physical need.

The Worst-Case (and Significantly More Likely) Scenario
All sexual positions are exhausted, and one of the Buck Fuddies realizes he or she no longer cares to share a duvet with someone who provides no physical, emotional, or intellectual satisfaction. Nevertheless, the 2 A.M. rendezvous continue until the other BF decides he or she is feeling used and/or wants more. There will be crying and/or door slamming, one last romp in the sack for old time's sake, and then, a baby. A beautiful, beautiful baby.

The "Opposites Attract"

How to Spot Them
Hipster indie rock chick with multiple tats kissing preppy Izod boy, and you're like, dude, has the whole world gone insane?

The Best-Case Scenario
Like Chris Robinson and Kate Hudson, they're just freaking cool.

The Worst-Case (and Significantly More Likely) Scenario
Julia Roberts and Lyle Lovett.

The "What's She Doing with Hims?"

How to Spot Them
One partner is significantly better looking, funnier, and/or smarter than the other. Typically, this means that the

less good looking, funny, and intelligent person has a giant . . . wallet, but sometimes there is no apparent explanation at all.

The Best-Case Scenario

The connection between these two is so deep that it doesn't matter if it can't be seen with the naked eye. The couple doesn't pay attention to the crooked glances and under-the-breath asides that follow them wherever they go—they're too busy building a life together based on mutual respect and their disdain for shallow people who gossip about couples they don't know. You know, people like us.

The Worst-Case (and Significantly More Likely) Scenario

She realizes that she could do much better, and she dumps him, and he knows the reason for the dumping. She then discovers that good-looking, smart guys are egomaniacs, and he realizes that he will never have sex with anyone as attractive as his ex again. Both are too proud to give it another go.

> One should always be in love.
> That's why one should never marry.
> —OSCAR WILDE

The "Best Friends"

How to Spot Them

Outwardly, they are the happiest of couples. They're playful; they're not overly sensitive to one another's teasing; they're easy to be around. They enjoy doing everything together, from shopping for groceries to spending holidays with each other's families. You know a couple fits this category if it seems impossible that either one could ever be with someone else.

The Best-Case Scenario

They break up. They read this book and learn that being alone has its perks, like having the bed to yourself and getting to see new people naked. The friendship, however, doesn't die. In fact, as friends, they are genuinely happy to help each other meet a new and better mate.

The Worst-Case (and Significantly More Likely) Scenario

The more they try to force passion, the more the friendship suffers. The relationship breaks up before anyone gets a chance to throw the friendship a life preserver. Since they never bothered to make friends with anybody else, they now have no friends or lovers.

Stages of Relationship Death

Nobody gets a soul mate. It don't happen.
All you going to get in life if you're lucky is a mate.
Somebody to fuck, go to movies with . . . that's all relationships are,
they're just fucking and eating . . . and the longer you're with someone,
there's more eating and less fucking.

—CHRIS ROCK

A relationship is like the Tour de France. There are a lot of peaks and valleys, periods of conserving your energy followed by reckless sprints, and finally the crushing realization that Lance Armstrong is going to win, not you. In short, there are a lot of stages.

Indeed, life is just a slow trot from Huggies to Depends, and every day in almost every relationship is just one day closer to "This isn't working."

So, how do two people go from cooing to "ew"-ing? Usually, it's gradual, although sometimes there's one dramatic moment that suddenly changes the entire relationship for the worse. These moments may or may not involve guns or strippers. Understanding the stages can help you get out of the relationship faster . . . and avoid both guns and strippers. The stages normally play out something like this:

Stage 1. Awkwardness

You meet someone and you start feeling things in your stomach that can't be relieved with ExLax. You want to reach out and touch her, but you don't know if she'd touch you back, or slap you.

Then she contacts you through MySpace! She does like you! Should you call? She left her number. Yes, you should call. You should definitely call. Shit. She's not answering. Do you leave a message? Beep. "Hi, Gina, it's Gary, from the other day. I just wanted to say . . ." What *did* you want to say? "Call me back"? Or "Let's go out sometime"? Or "Do you like music? 'Cause I love music, and bands that play music, and maybe sometime we could go see a band that plays music . . . together . . . or, separate, two cars, you know, whatever . . ."? The only thing to say

>))))— **My Worst Breakup** ⟶

by Molly Jong-Fast

In eleventh grade (age sixteen) I went out on two dates with Andrew Morgan (age twenty-four). He was the second (or third; depends on how you count) boy I ever kissed, and I fell madly in love with him despite or because of his enormous proboscis. He of course never called me back. I spent the year 1995 wandering around Second Avenue in New York (he lived above the grand yuppie coffeehouse DTUT), loitering/hooking outside of DTUT, hoping to catch a glimpse of my true love. Occasionally I would see him through the window making sweet love, or a pot of coffee, with other women. I began calling and hanging up on him. These were the joyous days before Caller ID. One day I was sitting in the coffee shop under his apartment when he emerged. I looked up at his bulbous nose, ready to fall into his arms and share all my feelings. "Andrew," I said. He paused. "You look familiar. Do you work at the Gap on Eighty-fourth?"

Molly Jong-Fast is the author of the novel *Normal Girl* and the memoir *The Sex Doctors in the Basement.*

———

about all this is that it's all just so . . . awkward. And hot. You spend two hours trying to think of what to write in an e-mail, and then you do it, and then you realize the other person probably could not have cared less what you said.

He/she either wants you, or he/she doesn't. She e-mails back. Oh my god! You both like music! You hang out, you have the obligatory first-date nonsense chatter (Where did you grow up? Where did you go to college? If you were a tree, what kind of tree would you be?). The number of siblings you have suddenly becomes information of utmost importance. Your evening ends when a self-conscious goodnight hug turns into a kiss and then turns into something that makes you wish you had a clean towel. This will inevitably lead to . . .

Stage 2: Being Annoying to All Your Friends

You used to take pride in your stoic aloneness, but all of a sudden you've become a cheerleader for love. Give me a G, give me an I, an N, an A, what's it spell? Gina! Have you met Gina? She is like *so* amazing. Life is so amazing! Where's that music coming from? You can hardly wait to get through the day so that you can see your shmoopie again, and you simply can't keep your mouth shut about it. The way she combs her hair, the stylish clothes she wears . . . is that from a song? Oh, who cares! Remember when you were out and you both started quoting the same movie at the same time?! Jinx, buy me a Coke! This wonderful life is just filled with bunnies and kittens and lollipops and scotch! Your friends are contemplating the fastest way to do away with you, but don't fret—before they can tie the noose you'll probably already be at . . .

Stage 3: Quiet Joy, Pleasing Rhythm

Mmm . . . quiet joy, pleasing rhythm. You've stopped extolling your new lover's virtues to whomever will listen, but that doesn't mean you've lost that loving feeling. Instead, it's grown. In fact, it's grown enough that you want to keep it to yourself. No one else can understand these feelings you're having. Weekends, you and your lover—the shape of his or her body still new—lay in bed together and talk about how great it is to not have to play games. You coo and cuddle and meow and make love and shower and make love again.

You call at least once a day to check in. You meet each other's families. It's a comfortable stage that can last a long time, but most of the time it will lull you into . . .

Stage 4: Monotony

The niceties have stopped. He no longer comes bearing flowers, or dinner reservations, or even movie passes. Midday checkup phone calls are made with less enthusiasm; you can hear him typing in the background. Suddenly questions arise, and they aren't the kind that get answered with a diamond. Didn't I just tell you that you don't look fat? Why do we spend so much of our time together doing laundry? Haven't we already done that position seven times this month? Didn't we just have this conversation?

Stage 5: Irritation

Stop nagging me! Seriously, stop it. I don't want to have dinner with your mother again, and I don't want to look at your pictures from Europe, again. Frankly, I don't even want to have sex with you (though I do want to have sex with your best friend). At first you try to overlook it, but then you can't help but visibly cringe every time he yawns on the phone, or pays for things with pennies, or spends a beautiful day indoors shredding old bank statements. Did she always slouch like that? Oh, and those pet names . . . not so cute anymore. Hoping to hold everything together a little longer, you gamely try to rise above that homicidal urge you're starting to feel whenever you hear your lover turn the doorknob or see him brush his teeth with your toothbrush. Before you know it, you're knocking on the door of . . .

> Am I the only person here who loves to watch a couple together that hates each other's guts?
>
> —DANE COOK,
> *RETALIATION*

Stage 6: Fighting

How come you never talk about how you're feeling! Why don't we ever make love anymore? Don't raise your voice at me! I'm not raising my voice! I'm perfectly calm! YOU'RE THE ONE WHO IS OUT OF CONTROL! I can't do this anymore! You're killing me! Wait . . . what are we even arguing about? The underlying subject matter of the spat might become clearer during . . .

Stage 7: Revelation

It's time to lay down your cards. During a long, possibly weepy talk, it might be revealed that you slept with someone else (but you used a condom . . . it broke, but you used a condom) or you just aren't sure you're ready for this kind of commitment (with this person) or you just can't deal with all the financial pressure you're under right now (and a new mate might have a fatter wallet). Often the revelation will be a blend of issues being expressed by both parties, and sometimes the mixture becomes so cloudy that no one is sure what the revelations are anymore. Or the revelation can be a purely internal one, where it suddenly dawns on you that the happiness ship has sailed without you. Either way, this is the moment when you're probably beginning to contemplate . . .

Stage 8: Figuring Out If It's Worth It

Is this as good as it gets? Are the issues in this relationship surmountable? You've both calmly stated your needs and wants . . . or perhaps you've just slammed doors in each other's faces and are now contemplating if you dislike this guy enough to kick him out and suck up having to pay the full rent. And buy new kitchen appliances. And go to weddings alone. Maybe it'd be easier to just mumble an apology and have makeup sex? Screw that. This body is cold, and it's time for . . .

Stage 9: The Breakup

Life is like a "Choose Your Own Adventure" book, and you've chosen to gamble that there's something better out there. But before you move on to the next chapter, you're going to have to cut the cord. For more on that, you'll have to read Part 2 of this book, which we promise will never, ever leave you. Of course, reading is lonely, and so you turn on the TV and you're watching a little Skinemax and drinking from that box of wine and now you want . . .

Stage 10: Makeup Sex

Ohhh baby, is this hot. Until you're lying there after, and he says the exact same thing that drove you insane in the first place, and now it's time for . . .

Stage 11: The Real Breakup

Turn to page 79.

> LAUREN CONRAD: "I don't want to marry Stephen."
> LAUREN BOSWORTH: "Why? He's cute.
>   You'd have pretty babies."
> JEN: "You *would* have pretty babies. Your babies
>   would be like the popular people at school."
> LAUREN CONRAD: "That's sweet."
>
> —*LAGUNA BEACH*

Is Your Relationship Kaput?
Take This Quiz and Find Out

I want a serious girlfriend.
Somebody I can love, that's gonna love me back. Is that psycho?
—JAKE, *SIXTEEN CANDLES*

Some people just can't take a hint. No matter how easy it is for friends, family, and fellow chat-room visitors to see that it's over, you or your lover refuse to take heed of the warning signs. In order to save time, not to mention unnecessary heartbreak, we humbly present you with a quiz to help you figure out if your relationship is through.

1) During lovemaking, your partner
   a) asks if you can finish after *The Real World/Road Rules Challenge*
   b) makes idle chitchat like, "Jenkins in accounting is a real douche. I don't understand why he keeps getting promoted."
   c) slurs his words because of the half bottle of bourbon consumed prior to the act
   d) asks if you can spice up your sex life by adding other people
   e) doesn't say anything, because the phrase "during lovemaking" does not apply to your relationship

2) On your birthday, your lover gives you
   a) a gift from Office Depot, and you think this is an improvement, because last year's gift was from the 99 Cent store
   b) divorce papers
   c) a vibrator
   d) a scale
   e) the same thing you gave him for his birthday

3) Your significant other signs his/her e-mails
   a) Best wishes,
   b) Many thanks,
   c) Smell you later,
   d) May the force be with you,
   e) Peace out, bitches,

4) When you go out to eat, your partner
   a) says, "So we're going dutch, right?"
   b) points out that the Caesar salad might not be a wise choice for someone with so much "junk in the trunk"
   c) asks your feelings about open relationships
   d) makes passive-aggressive comments, "Oh, so now you swallow"
   e) asks the waitress what time she gets off

5) You call your significant other, and
   a) you say, "It's me," and he says, "Can you be more specific?"
   b) the call costs $5.99 per minute
   c) he breathes heavily into the phone, then hangs up
   d) he says, "I'll call you back. . . . Can I get your number?"
   e) he makes a clicking sound with his tongue, then says he is getting a call on the other line

In order to find out whether the fat lady has sung on your relationship, give yourself three points for every time you answered *c* or *d,* then multiply this number by six, then divide by four, then take the square root. If this number is greater than pi, you are in the perfect relationship.

Just kidding!

If you selected any of the choices to any of these questions, your relationship is over. But don't worry—there's something better around the bend: excessive masturbation.

YOUR ACTUAL SCORE:
FAILED-RELATIONSHIP QUOTIENT

Okay, okay, we know: we tricked you. You wanted some kind of real numerical relationship score that would magically tell you what percentage chance there is that your relationship is or isn't going to make it, and we didn't deliver.

Sorry! SORRY! Jeez.

We'll make it up to you here.

Here's how to find out your Failed-Relationship Quotient.

Got that calculator ready?

Step 1: Count the total number of failed romantic relationships you've been in. Start from as early as you can remember, and count every relationship regardless of how long it lasted. As unfair as it might seem, a one-night stand and a five-year marriage count the same here. For the purposes of this calculation, a failed relationship is any one that ended. Math leaves no room for all that "but it wasn't really a failure because I learned something" stuff. If it ended because your lover died, we leave it to you to interpret that as a success or a failure. If you're still in a relationship, it isn't a failure (even if it feels like one).

Step 2: Count the total number of relationships you've had. As before, you must count every relationship regardless of length.

Step 3: Divide the first number by the second number, and multiply the answer by one hundred.

Your romantic failure rate =
(Failed relationships / total relationships) x 100

YOUR SCORE:

100 percent: You're perfect . . . perfectly normal, that is. In relationships you've done nothing but fail, and now you are alone. But isn't it nice to have something in your life at which you're so consistent?

99–51 percent: Okay, okay, you've had some relationship successes, but you're no breakup novice either. We're 92 percent sure you'll get to 100 percent soon.

50 percent or less: You're lying, either to yourself or to the person you're cheating on. Or both.

He's Not Cheating, He Just Works a Lot: The Cheaty McCheats a Lot Chart

Oh, don't cry.

I'm so sorry I cheated so much, but that's the way things are.

—DOLORES "LOLITA" HAZE, *LOLITA*

Because few breakups are completely "divorced" from the presence of Someone Else, we've documented the common cheaters' catch phrases, translated them, and then suggested some ways to thwart his or her attempts to be unfaithful.

Your cheater says:	Is actually . . .	You need to . . .
"I'm working late."	On a date with the intern from work, or actually at work, banging said intern.	Announce you are "working late" too, and then come home with your shirt buttons misaligned, or, better yet, don't come home at all.
"I'm not spending excessive time online—I'm just catching up on some notes."	E-mailing a new lover or servicing his addiction to Internet porn while e-mailing a new lover.	Sign your lover up for absurd amounts of spam, so that he can't log on without getting a message from Miss Kitty257.
"The only reason you saw Match.com open on my computer was because I was looking for someone for my brother to date."	To paraphrase the great Nick Twisp, looking to place his wendell in a winkie.	Do a search on the dating site for everyone in the range of your cheater's height and age in your general area, and see if you can find his or her profile. If that doesn't work (your cheater may have

Your cheater says:	Is actually . . .	You need to . . .
		hidden the profile by saying he/she lives in Montana or something), sign up for the service yourself.
"I don't smell like anything. Stop accusing me."	Lying like the cheap hooker he (or she) just banged.	Put on men's cologne (a kind your cheater doesn't wear) and when he says something, exclaim, "Stop accusing me!"
"I brought you these flowers."	Feeling guilty for diddling the girl at Starbuck's.	Tell him to give the flowers "to your whore."
"I joined the gym because I want to get in shape."	Joining the gym in order to look good naked for a new lover.	Join the gym too, not to spy but to get in even better shape than your cheater.
"I was stuck in traffic."	Was involved in a serious affair that could lead to marriage.	Check the traffic report on the radio in order to reveal the lie. Or else simply hide the keys to prevent any possible future driving.
"I'm too tired to make love."	Tired from having already made love, to someone else.	Tell her that making love to her while she's sleeping won't seem so different than doing it when she's awake.
"Those are the cleaning lady's earrings."	Doing someone else in your bed.	Wash the sheets in itching powder.

The guy was stabbed. . . .
It turns out it was his ex-girlfriend [who did it]. . . .
Think about it, Jerry:
There is something exciting about this guy
if he can arouse that kind of passion.
—ELAINE, *SEINFELD*

The Relationship Survey Results

My wife, Mary, and I have been married for forty-seven years
and not once have we had an argument bad enough to consider divorce;
murder, yes, but divorce, never.
—JACK BENNY

Look out, Kinsey: we polled hundreds of people of all ages about their experiences in the dating fishbowl. So the next time your friend asks if it's normal that she and her boyfriend have sex only on major holidays and when the Tivo is broken, you'll have a scientific answer.

How long would you say your average romantic relationship has lasted?

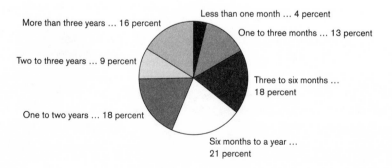

More than three years ... 16 percent

Less than one month ... 4 percent

One to three months ... 13 percent

Two to three years ... 9 percent

Three to six months ... 18 percent

One to two years ... 18 percent

Six months to a year ... 21 percent

)))— **My First Breakup** ⟶

by Andrea Seigel

Throughout fifth and sixth grade, I had an on-again, off-again relationship with Brian Millat. We were in the gifted class. That means we were intellectually gifted, not physically handicapped. We were not, however, gifted enough to figure out how to see each other after school got out. I did not know what Brian looked like post–3 P.M. During school hours, though, we square-danced, not because we were complete dorks but because the school required it. And we carved "I LOVE [insert each other's names]" into our desks, although we never said "I love you" to each other's faces.

We had our ups and downs. One of the ups being that we liked to touch knees while hearing about the Gulf War during "Current Events" time. One of the downs being that I heard through the grapevine that Brian thought I was prettier with my hair in a ponytail, and since I mostly wore it down, this information totally messed me up.

At the graduation dance, we kissed for the very first time. There were many familiar moms chaperoning the dance, and I was convinced that seeing this kiss, they now believed I was a slut. I was wearing the sixth-grade version of a bustier that night, and this reaction is exactly what I was going for. Brian and I didn't so much dance that night as hug, putting our heads on each other's shoulders, never breaking. We didn't talk. It took us about three hours to kiss, with Brian initiating. Just as I hadn't figured out that

(continues)

relationships extended beyond the classroom, I hadn't figured out that I could touch him with something other than my knee. And I did not even use my knee well. I know that now, having watched professional lap dancers on HBO.

I do not remember an actual good-bye. I know that Brian wrote "I love you" in cursive in the back of my yearbook, but in my mind there's no moment where we looked at each other, realized that sixth grade was over, and made our peace with the damage. All I remember is going home in my parents' car, being given a mood ring/watch, and then going to see Kevin Costner in *Robin Hood: Prince of Thieves.*

The summer went by.

I can't even pinpoint the day when the breakup occurred. There was never a decision made out loud or on paper, and there was never an event that marked the change between us. I can say that I don't think the breakup was that day that we said good-bye. And I don't think it was the day that I showed up for my first day of seventh grade and couldn't bring myself to say hi to him. I think it happened on some day in the middle of that summer, a day blended into the rest, and so my very first breakup wasn't a specific incident locked down in time, but instead an invisible shift. There must have been an almost silent crack in my brain while I was swimming or sleeping or buying a new backpack that registered, "And now it's over."

We had an orientation assembly on that first day of middle school, and I remember looking at the back of Brian's head during it. He was about ten rows in front of me. I think he knew I was behind him. I think we were scared to look at each other because what we had to talk about was impossible to talk about. I stared at the place where his hair met his neck—he had gotten a haircut recently—and what I felt was that I didn't have access to him anymore. One of the worst phrases I've ever heard is "growing apart" because "growing" implies something good.

Our breakup never produced any tears or physical thrashing, as later breakups have done. But what it did was introduce me to the heartbreak of adulthood, which in my world has been the fact that distance creeps in, and you can never remember when or where or how. No matter how hard you try to stop it, by the time you've become aware that you're losing, it's already happened. Before Brian, I had never imagined that something as stupid as falling out of contact could ever hurt the bond between two people. That's his legacy in my life, and that's also why when I run into him every once in a while, I feel a belated twinge when we separate.

Andrea Seigel is the author of *Like the Red Panda* and the forthcoming *To Feel Stuff*.

There's nothing like unrequited love

to take all the flavor out of a

peanut butter sandwich.

—CHARLIE BROWN

What do you think is the ideal age to settle down?

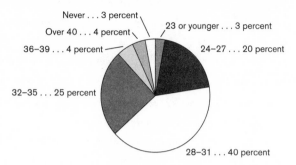

Never . . . 3 percent
Over 40 . . . 4 percent
36–39 . . . 4 percent
32–35 . . . 25 percent
23 or younger . . . 3 percent
24–27 . . . 20 percent
28–31 . . . 40 percent

How long does the "honeymoon period" usually last in your relationship?

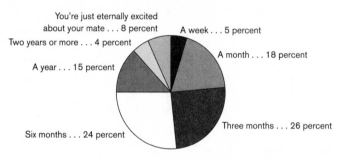

You're just eternally excited about your mate . . . 8 percent
Two years or more . . . 4 percent
A year . . . 15 percent
Six months . . . 24 percent
A week . . . 5 percent
A month . . . 18 percent
Three months . . . 26 percent

I did the following in my last serious relationship:

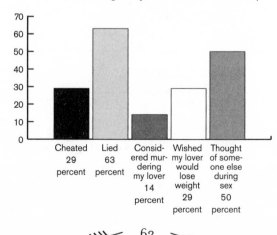

| Cheated 29 percent | Lied 63 percent | Considering murdering my lover 14 percent | Wished my lover would lose weight 29 percent | Thought of someone else during sex 50 percent |

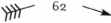

If you ever cheated on a lover, did you:

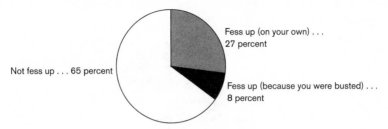

Fess up (on your own) . . .
27 percent

Not fess up . . . 65 percent

Fess up (because you were busted) . . .
8 percent

The thing(s) I hate most about being in a relationship is:

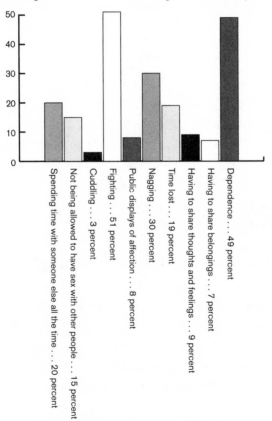

Spending time with someone else all the time . . . 20 percent
Not being allowed to have sex with other people . . . 15 percent
Cuddling . . . 3 percent
Fighting . . . 51 percent
Public displays of affection . . . 8 percent
Nagging . . . 30 percent
Time lost . . . 19 percent
Having to share thoughts and feelings . . . 9 percent
Having to share belongings . . . 7 percent
Dependence . . . 49 percent

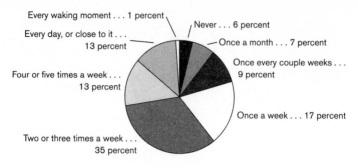

In your last relationship, how often did you have sex?

Every waking moment . . . 1 percent

Never . . . 6 percent

Every day, or close to it . . . 13 percent

Once a month . . . 7 percent

Once every couple weeks . . . 9 percent

Four or five times a week . . . 13 percent

Once a week . . . 17 percent

Two or three times a week . . . 35 percent

From the Trenches:
I Knew It Was Over When . . .

We asked people who'd experimented with "relationships" what kind of hints there were that their last romance was heading for the hills. Here are a few of their responses.

"I knew he wasn't in love with me when he said that he was going to get inside my head and break me down." Cecilia, 33

"I found myself getting irritated with him all the time. It got so I just didn't even want him around me, not touching me, not talking to me. It was grad- ual, but then one day I realized I would be happy never seeing him again." Barbara, 45

"I knew he wasn't in love with me when he said he would rather sleep at his mother's house on New Year's Eve than at mine." Ronda, 27

"I realized she'd rather be with a black guy than my white ass." Tom, 25

"I should've known he was no longer into it when he started to say things like 'Whatever happens between us, I don't want you to ever twist things around and say I never loved you.' But actually, I guess I could say I didn't finally know my ex was really and truly no longer in love with me until I heard he was engaged to an ex friend of mine." Heather, 29

"I knew I was no longer in love with her (as if I ever was in the first place) when I came to the realization one day that I'd much rather smoke pot and swim some laps in the pool than sit around watching her gaze at the television and pack on pounds." Hugh, 25

"He started feeling like the brother I'd never had." Molly, 24

"I knew we were on the outs when she said, 'If I'm not with someone who wants kids by the time I'm thirty-five, I'm having them myself,' and I said, 'I don't want them.'" Dan, 33

"I knew I wasn't in love anymore when, as lonely as I was sitting at home by myself without a job, just the thought of him coming through the door at the end of the day made me nauseated. It made me feel like I wanted to lock myself in the bathroom for the rest of the night." Sara, 31

"Once he went to jail, I was pretty sure I was no longer in love." Molly, 26

"I realized he was no longer in love with me when he would stay up all night viewing Internet porn instead of coming to bed." Jane, 24

"He was no longer as thoughtful, called less often, didn't send me e-mails at work." Jennifer, 29

"She just started looking at me differently." Jessica, 29

"I started doubting my feelings of love when I realized I would look at other men in a romantic manner. I would think, 'I wonder what it would be like to date him.'" Marianna, 22

"I knew I didn't love him because he cheated on me and gave me herpes. He then lied about the herpes and slept with my best friend." Courtney, 22

"It was over once we got married. After we got married, I realized the only reason we'd gotten married was because I was pissed off it had taken so long for us to get married and we were only really doing it because our families were pressuring us ridiculously." Heather, 24

"I went to visit my family without him, and I was so happy to be away from him I realized something must be wrong." Lauren, 25

"He stopped reaching for my hand when we'd walk." Ashley, 35

"When my boyfriend came home from a strip club in the middle of the night, woke me up, and said he thought it would be a good idea if I moved out, I knew he was no longer in love with me." Michelle, 31

"I fell out of love when I called him in tears because I'd found out my father wasn't really my father, and he just continued to sit on his stoop smoking weed with his friends." Mollie, 24

"I sensed he wasn't into me when he said he wanted to try dating a blonde because he'd never dated a blonde before (I am a brunette). Then he made a disparaging comment while I was giving him a blow job, and that was that." Tiffany, 34

"I felt trapped." Gabrielle, 29

WHAT NOT TO DO AFTER A BREAKUP

Don't . . . light yourself on fire.

But no one would ever do that! Or would they?

According to the *Alabama Mobile Register,* on May 14, 2005, twenty-one-year-old Robert McCants threw a tantrum while he and his girlfriend were discussing their relationship's plight at an Alabama gas station. The fight ended when McCants doused himself in gasoline and set himself on fire. The good news is he was okay. The bad news is not only has he felt like an idiot ever since but he's smelled like one, too.

How about instead of doing this, you try:

Savagely burning . . . the tip of a cigarette.

"To quote Pink Floyd, 'comfortably numb.' I would look at her and feel nothing." Frank, 30

"I knew I wasn't in love anymore when I would look at him and become physically ill." Barbara, 30

"I knew it was over when my lover of two years said I wasn't his 'ideal scene.'" Jan, 51

"He started going through this second teenagerdom thing and joined a band at age thirty-three, saying he wanted to 'become a rock star.'" Teresa, 38

"I said, 'I love you,' and he said, 'That's nice.'" Daisy, 25

"I knew I wasn't in like with my ex (I never loved her) when she became so annoying that the sex and head and great breasts just made me sick to think about." Josh, 19

THE CEREAL THEORY OF RELATIONSHIPS: WHY YOU CAN'T MARRY COOKIE CRISP

Do you ever feel like shopping for a mate is painfully similar to shopping for cereal? It wasn't always so. In past generations, the hungry picked Cheerios or Corn Flakes and ate them for breakfast, every day. It wasn't about finding the perfect cereal. It was about making a choice that was good for you and accepting it.

But walk into a supermarket today and it's difficult not to be paralyzed by choice. With so many cereals—every taste, texture, and crunch (not to mention all those little toys like the Wobbler!)—how to pick just one? Sure, Cookie Crisp is delicious, the way it leaves even the milk sweeter, but let's be honest: Cookie Crisp is a slut; you can't take Cookie Crisp home to your family. Raisin Bran is kind and dependable, but do you want to spend the rest of your life with Raisin Bran? The fact is, sometimes you want the Crisp, and sometimes you want the Bran, and sometimes you have a few too many drinks and want the Crisp and the Bran at the same time. The more choices we have, the more difficult it becomes to choose. And the more we hold out for the perfect cereal, the less likely we may be to find it.

So next time you go to the supermarket or the bar, close your eyes, point, and choose, and see whether you're still in the mood for Wheaties the next morning or you're wishing you had gone Fruit Loops.

"I could no longer just hang out with the girls without him tagging along in order to start an argument." Rose, 21

"I knew he didn't care when we were messing around and he didn't 'get off.'" Hannah, 18

"I got the feeling that he was no longer interested when we would hang out once or twice a week and after every time he'd say, 'I'm going to need some time to myself next week.'" Rina, 18

"The desire for other women became stronger than my desire for my girl." Brett, 23

"I noticed that he was out of love with me when he stopped calling me pet names and just called me by my first name. And he didn't seem excited to cuddle with me or hold my hand anymore." Tiffany, 27

"I had a car crash and he never bothered to call to see if I was okay." Sarah, 24

"I realized I wasn't really in love anymore when we were at a wedding to-gether—I knew no one but the bride and groom—and I was sitting there thinking I would be having more fun if I was there by myself." Caroline, 25

"It was obvious when he said, 'This is probably the last thing you'll ever hear me say.'" Samantha, 31

"I knew I was no longer in love when I started seeing him as a roommate rather than my boyfriend. He had no interest in anything physical." Sarah, 29

"I knew I was no longer in love when I looked her in the eye and thought, 'You're a nasty, manipulative liar and I don't think you're capable of being a good person.'" Bell, 22

"She told me she was straight." Christina, 37

Everything Else You Ever Wanted to Know about Relationships (but Were Afraid to Ask Dr. Phil)

Who better to ask about relationship failure than two people who have systematically messed up every romantic affair they've had? Because every breakup must be preceded by a relationship, many people have quizzed us on our views about getting involved with someone in the first place (to quote Damon Wayans on *In Living Color,* "hated it"). Here are our answers to the most frequently asked questions.

The only solid and lasting peace between a man and his wife is, doubtless, a separation.
—LORD CHESTERFIELD

Can two people ever just meet, like each other the same amount, and live happily ever after, or is every relationship doomed to unravel?

FLINT: 99.9 percent of human relationships are doomed. There are exceptions to every rule, such as couples with extremely low expectations. You know, those people who join Internet dating sites and marry their semi-blind first date. They claim that it was just serendipity, but let's be honest: it's just low standards. So yes, two people can meet, like each other the same amount, and live happily ever after. But most of these are the kind of people who could marry a Chia Pet and live happily ever after.

ANNA JANE: Every now and then a relationship can be truly happy, but happily ever after is never really as happy as it looks. Most relationships are doomed, except in cases of death. Romeo and Juliet? Very in love, and very dead very young. That might be why they never had to worry about divvying up the Tiffany goblets.

What's the key to a healthy relationship?

FLINT: A lot of love, a lot of lies, and a lot of distractions, like kids or season tickets to the Met (or to see the Mets). Cherish your significant other. Never berate her, never yell at her, never tell her not to eat a second slice of cheesecake. Make sure she knows you would run in front of a moving train for her. Yet keep your own interests and your own hobbies. Don't share everything with your mate. Don't spend all your time with your mate. Have crushes on other people. My uncle Herb and aunt Estelle are the happiest couple I know. They're in their eighties, and magnificently young, attractive, smart, and vibrant. What's their secret, according to the people who know them best? They split a bottle of gin every night.

ANNA JANE: Well said, Flint. The real question is: with such insight into successful coupling, why can't you ever keep a girlfriend?

FLINT: Problems in the sack.

Is there a secret to successful cheating?

ANNA JANE: No. Even if you manage to cheat without the other person finding out, it will sully your conscience long after the relationship is over, and that's going to make it hard for you to view it as a success in the long run.

FLINT: Conscience? Do men have those? Yes, there is a secret to successful cheating. Make sure your significant other can never ever find out. Play six degrees of separation in your head. If you can link the person you're about to bed with the person you're about to wed, don't do it.

I think people should mate for life, like pigeons or Catholics.
—ISAAC DAVIS,
MANHATTAN

If your lover cheats on you and you decide to stay with him or her anyway, can you continue to hold it against him or her?

FLINT: No. If you have decided to take your boyfriend back and forgive him for sleeping with, say, Jenny, you can't six months later be like, "Sweetie, why didn't you take out the garbage, and WHY DID YOU PUT YOUR PENIS IN JENNY?" If you're the jealous, rage-filled type, don't take your lover back after adultery.

ANNA JANE: But you get permission to hold it against your lover if he ever does it again.

FLINT: There should never be a second time. Think of your relationship like you think of your member of Congress. Every couple years, there needs to be a midterm evaluation. If they haven't done their job, get someone else in there that can.

Can you casually date someone, or does this always lead to one party getting hurt?

FLINT: It always leads to one party getting hurt. This isn't to say one shouldn't do it anyway, but be aware of the consequences, and don't fool yourself into thinking that the other person is as casual as you are, or that sex doesn't complicate things.

ANNA JANE: Yes. One person always thinks things are more serious than the other person is willing to believe.

Anna Jane, as a former wedding columnist, how do weddings make you feel?

ANNA JANE: Jealous.

FLINT: Every time I see two people get married, a part of me dies. I mean, can they be any more cliché? Do something original, people. Oh, wait, no one asked me, did they? My bad.

When things get hard in a relationship, how do I know if it's worth it to try to work things out or if I'm better off just leaving?

FLINT: Like most guys, I struggle with the "Is it worth it?" question every day of a relationship. I love having someone to laugh with, someone to go to a movie with, someone to play ping-pong with, but there are so many things that weigh on me. Do we have enough to say to one another? Is this silence comfortable or an indication that we've run out of things to say, on the third date?

In my adult dating life, I've been in the following situations: being with someone I love but am not in love with (in the passionate sense), being in love with someone who refused to love me back, and being in love with someone whose family I could not stand. Each of these situations raises a different series of questions. Can passion be found? Is the basis for a good relationship friendship or romance or both? When you find what you feel is true love but it's unrequited, how long do you wait for the other person to come around?

Everyone has a different threshold of "Is it worth it?" For me, it's not worth it if the person I'm dating yells, is an accountant, weighs more than I do, prays regularly, can't go anywhere without me, has jealousy issues, doesn't want kids, wants too many kids, doesn't read the Sunday *New York Times,* reads only the Travel section of the Sunday *Times,* doesn't like to read but owns books on tape, or doesn't think it's adorable when she asks why we can't spend more time together and I say, quoting Pee Wee Herman, "I'm a loner, Dottie, a rebel."

Most important, though, I won't date someone who doesn't pass the "breakfast table test." If I can imagine sitting at the breakfast table with someone, thirty years from now, and it makes me smile, then I know it's worth it.

ANNA JANE: First of all, I think I should point out that I've never cleared the "Is it worth it?" hurdle; either I've decided someone didn't warrant the work that needs to be poured into a relationship in order to sustain it or someone has foolishly decided I wasn't worth it.

What I feel Flint's answer lacks is consideration for unsexy relationship issues, like money and children. I think when one or both of these factors become seriously intertwined in a relationship, the dynamics change. With higher stakes, it can be harder to judge whether everything is worth tossing out just because at the moment you're really disliking the person you're with. Of course, you could always just decide to keep your lover and toss the money and children . . .

That said, I really like parts of Flint's answer. Yes, ideally you should beam at the thought of one day sharing denture cream with the person you're currently banging. I think it's also worth it if you know you'd want to be with the person no matter what. How would you feel if you learned your lover was paralyzed, or Republican?

Is it possible to really love someone, but not want to be in a relationship with him or her?

ANNA JANE: Yes. I've been told so during many a breakup.

FLINT: Oh, Anna Jane, sweet, sweet Anna Jane. Men invented this lie to make women feel better about the fact they're getting dumped. I'm so sorry.

>>>— **My Worst Breakup** ——>

by Kerri Pomarolli

Okay, picture it: 1993, the Sigma Nu fraternity house, Prince setting the mood. Our eyes met across the dance floor. Dan Klesman was a legend on campus. My sorority sisters used to say, "Could we have a moment of silence for Dan Klesman's abs?" He was hot redefined. I couldn't believe that I was dancing with him, and, as he walked me home in the freezing snow, we sang our hearts out to Journey and REO Speedwagon. He was as cheesy as I was. I had found my soul mate.

We started our love affair immediately, but he always said he had to study so we could only see each other on Monday and Wednesday nights. He was always at the library. One night I insisted he take me with him on a "study date," and he agreed. The thing was, being a musical theater major I didn't have any books, so I borrowed some, found the undergraduate library, and met him there.

We walked in and the silence was deafening. The next thing you know we were standing in front of one cold cubicle. He said, "See ya in a few hours," and then he walked away. This was not quite the night I had imagined. I sat there writing "Mrs. Dan Klesman" and waiting. An hour passed, two hours, three hours. I didn't know if he forgot about me or was trying to send a message, but he never came back, and that was the end of our affair.

Years later I was at our college reunion and I met this great girl whom I never knew in college. It turned out that we had a lot of friends in common. We found out we both knew and even dated the infamous Dan Klesman. I said, "Yeah, it was 1993, first semester." Her mouth dropped. "Me too! But he was always studying, so I could only see him on Tuesdays and Thursdays."

Kerri Pomarolli is a stand-up comedian and the author of *If I'm Waiting on God, Then What Am I Doing in a Christian Chatroom?*

PART TWO

The Breakup

I gave her my heart,
and she gave me a pen.
—LLOYD DOBLER,
SAY ANYTHING

There's something amazing that tends to happen when two people fall in love: they grow, they change, and, eventually, they come to hate each other.

Sure, some will learn to cope with daily feelings of utter disgust; others will work past the hatred only to grow stronger and then rub their triumph in their friends' faces; a brave few will distract themselves by procreating.

However, for the vast majority of us, when love packs its bags and loathing settles in, it means there's a breakup in our near future.

And this fills us with unimaginable fear. Will he refuse to let me break up with him? Will she post those nudie pics I gave her on the Internet? Will he attack me with a soup-spoon? Am I making a huge mistake?

But fear no longer, for today, we shall break down breakups until you learn to love them and long for them in the way you once longed for your partner's naked, hairy body.

Breakups shouldn't be scary. The truth is, we knew deep down it was coming all along. This is the moment the relationship was building up to. It's an event that, in spite of ourselves, we've long imagined; it's a moment we'll be replaying in our minds for months or even years to come.

And it's also something we might as well get good at doing because the majority of the relationships on which we embark will fail. Love and sitcom pilots have about the same success rate.

Yet most of us are shocked when they don't work out.

Take our good friend Jackie. Not so long ago, Jackie was a strong, successful, confident woman—optimistic to her core. Today, she is a blubbering wreck, a real human

mashed potato. Chapped lips. Distended belly. Inappropriate relationship with her cats.

How did she go from superwoman to potato woman? A little thing called the breakup. It hit Jackie with the force of a Shaquille O'Neal dunk, of a Jessica Simpson vocal gone terribly wrong. It hurt. It really, really hurt, and poor Jackie is firmly convinced she will never love again. She's sure that the love boat has sailed for the last time, and she never even got to meet Captain Stubing.

It doesn't matter if her ex was five foot three and had halitosis and was in a band that never got a gig.

It's not that Jackie misses this garlic-munching, banjo-strumming, unemployment-receiving loser so much as she misses having someone to sing to her and breathe garlic on her and tickle her to sleep.

Like Jackie, we've all been through at least one messy, bloody, lingering breakup. Yet no matter how many times we go through it, we never seem to get it right. Every time, we seem to say the wrong thing, act the wrong way, make a wrong pass at the wrong person at the wrong bar, and then make the wrong morning-after call when we realize our mistake.

The problem is, we assume that we have to fail at the breakup just because we failed at the relationship. We are all used to failing at the breakup. We take it for granted.

Why? The reason is simple: we're taught that it's something to be ashamed of, something not to talk about.

In a society obsessed with soul mates, breakups are the elephants that won't leave the room. In the movies, John Cusack holding up a boom box in the rain makes him the perfect romantic. In life, it makes him a stalker. On *The*

O.C., awkward Seth Cohen, obsessed with comic books, is geek chic, and gets the girl of his dreams. In high schools all across America, Seth Cohen is getting beat up and dumped, while the guy who beat him up is knocking boots with a busty blonde.

In the following pages, we will attempt to strip the elephant naked, to poke and prod the body of the great beast, to ridicule it, to try to make the elephant dance.

In a culture that celebrates moments of transformation—graduations, births, weddings—we haven't learned to celebrate the good-byes. So, let's give the breakup the same amount of respect we give other ceremonies. It doesn't need to be hurried or ignored. Instead, it should be embraced, chewed over, analyzed until the wee hours of the mornings.

When it's truly over, you're going to be allowed to mourn or revel as you please.

But leading up to that point, you want your arsenal full. Do you have the right vocabulary to get through this period? Do you have a plan of attack in mind? Do you know how to give in to the pain, because you're going to need to live it, love it in the same way that you loved the person that's exiting your life?

Like a driving rain on a bitterly cold night, breaking up sucks, but it is also kind of wonderful, because it reminds you that you're alive. Alive enough to care that you're alone. Remember, without life's lows, drinking wouldn't be as much fun.

So come with us, and let's see how low we can go before we stop blaming ourselves. Because even if we really are to blame, it's going to be a lot easier to deal with the hurt if we decide the problem wasn't us—it was them.

PROFILES IN NOT-A-LOT-OF-COURAGE

Terrifica

It's a bird! It's a plane! It's . . . Terrifica?

Stalking the streets of NYC, Terrifica's mission is to save drunk women in bars from having their hearts broken by assholes.

By day Terrifica is a computer technician named Sarah (she won't reveal her real last name), but, by night, she wears a red cape and a blonde wig and becomes a selfless, ersatz Wonder Woman who patrols bars and pulls ladies out of sticky situations when they are too feeble to fight for themselves. "Women are weak. They are easily manipulated, and they need to be protected from themselves and most certainly from men and their ill intentions toward them," she told ABC News.

On hand at all times she keeps lipstick, a camera, a cell phone, pepper spray, and Smarties (the food from which she gets her energy, she says). Her superpower is her sobriety; most men are too drunk to fight her off when she shows up to tug away their potential lay.

"To feel like you have to go to a bar, to put yourself out there, feeling like you have worth only when you're married, engaged, or have a boyfriend, that's weakness. People are happiest when they're alone and living their solitary lives," she said.

Originally from Pittsburgh, Sarah became Terrifica after getting her heart broken upon moving to New York a decade ago.

In the ensuing years, she's become an expert on fending off heartbreak, but that doesn't mean her own broken heart has been mended. "The reason why Batman was dark was because he kept seeing his demon [the murder of his parents and his need to avenge them] every time he did what he did," she told ABC. "I guess that is essentially the same thing with me. I experience the same hurt and pain over and over again [as Terrifica]."

The Breakup Glossary

NANCY: *"I just don't think we should see each other anymore,*
it has nothing to do with the fact that you're short,
and it has nothing to do with the fact that you're not bright enough."
FIELDING MELLISH: *"I don't understand. Do you have fun*
when you're with me?"
NANCY: *"No. But it's not that."*

—*BANANAS*

After you've exhausted phrases like "monkey torture" and "castration isn't good enough for that bastard," you'll need a vocabulary that truly captures your irrational moods and reactions.

What you'll need is a breakup glossary.

Albatross
The possessions of your ex that you don't want to keep after the breakup, but don't want to give back either. If he smashed your heart, do you smash his spice rack? Like the dead bird the Ancient Mariner is forced to wear around his neck as punishment in that long poem we pretended to read in high school, albatrosses just can't be shaken off. Common ones include Joni Mitchell CDs, sofas, iMacs, Gap hoodies, and dogs.

Angry Dating
A technique employed mainly but not exclusively by men in which the recently dumped treat dates/new lovers terri-

bly, as if this will somehow get back at the ex who treated them badly.

Antiquing
Systematically going back and sleeping with everyone you've ever dated, also known as being a desperate whore.

Automatic Updates
Trying to make sure your exes see that you're better off without them by needlessly including them in large group e-mails containing new job contact information, or photos of you looking incredible, preferably standing next to someone taller and more gorgeous than any of your exes ever were.

Blue Binning
(Also known as "Recycling")
Dating someone you've broken up with before, mainly because it's convenient and because it doesn't increase the total number of sexual partners you've had.

Breakup Sex
Coitus with a party immediately following the agreement to sever romantic ties, often confused by the more amorous party as being makeup sex. Typically, breakup sex is the best sex ever experienced in the relationship, and thus makes you reevaluate the entire breakup. Of course, this begs the

question: do we break up in order to introduce good sex into our relationship, or do we have good sex because we're relieved to be through with the jerk?

Coitus Hiatus (CH)

The break from sex that sometimes occurs after a breakup. CH can be voluntary or involuntary, and we highly recommend it, unless you meet someone amazing, or you're extremely drunk, or it's Saturday night.

Cubic Zirconium

The stone with which a woman replaces the diamond in her engagement ring before returning it to her fiancé. Pro-

---

WHAT NOT TO DO AFTER A BREAKUP

Don't . . . throw furniture out the window.

But no one would ever do that! Or would they?

In March 2005, a twenty-one-year-old Hong Kong resident named Hu Wu was dumped by his girlfriend and chose to take out his frustration on the poor helpless sidewalk by tossing furniture at it from his window. Unfortunately, he lived in a thirty-fifth-floor apartment. We have a feeling that the condo board did not approve. According to local news reports, no one was hurt. However, the family was in serious need of an Ikea run: all that was left in the apartment was an air conditioner, a fridge, and a washing machine.

How about instead of doing this, you try:

Writing awful things about your ex on paper airplanes and then launching them from your roof.

---

ceeds from selling the original stone are often used by the former fiancée to buy Vibratex Rabbit vibrators for herself and her eighty-seven closest friends.

Dog Catching
Catching your ex with his or her current flame, only to discover that the new love is a real dog. Dog catching tends to make you feel better at first (she'll regret breaking up with me forever!), until it dawns on you that you might unknowingly be a dog too, and your ex's new lover is actually a step up.

Drunk Dialing
Grandfather of drunk texting, drunk e-mailing, and drunk faxing.

Dumpee
He or she who is dumped.

Dumper
He or she who does the dumping.

ExBay
Online auctions where scorned parties sell their ex's belongings. This is often done as an attempt to raise funds to

pay off legal fees, or to profit at the cost of an ex's public humiliation.

Ex Sex
Postrelationship nookie with a recently ditched lover, often the result of the epiphany that you might never have sex with anyone else again . . . for free.

Guyatus
The period when a woman takes a break from men after a relationship ends. Popular activities during the guyatus include knitting, gaining weight, getting a dog, joining book clubs, and discussing how awful guys are . . . and how much you miss your ex.

Hand
As in "the upper hand," or the dominant member of a relationship. The funny thing about "hand" is that it can change, er, hands, after the breakup, when one party realizes that he or she made a tragic mistake.

Married Friends
Your friends that have gone over to the dark side and no longer speak the language of normal people. They have condos and babies and only speak in the "royal we," even when answering e-vites that were addressed to only one person.

Mostly Single
If you're in a long-distance relationship or if you've been seeing someone for more than three months but haven't yet committed, you're neither single nor in a relationship. Instead, you're "mostly single."

Mostly Dead
Married.

Outsourcing
No, it's not sending your ex to India (though that's not a bad idea). It's diversifying your love life so as to minimize the emotional damage any single break can do. A good outsourcer would have one partner for hanging out (someone gay if you're straight), one to have casual sex with, one to have an emotional connection with, and one who will buy you stuff.

Payback Sack
The art of sleeping with anyone and everyone your ex has cared for, including his (or her) family, friends, hairdresser, and rabbi.

Prep Wife
A woman who finds that her ex-boyfriends always marry the next person they date after the breakup. She will most likely also be someone who incessantly talks about this

uncanny trend in her love life, a habit that will only further ensure that she'll forever remain the appetizer and never become the main course.

PTBS (Post-traumatic Breakup Syndrome)

A malady often suffered when one is having difficulty moving on after a bad breakup. Symptoms may include loss of appetite for anything but Nutella, spontaneous sobbing on buses, repetition of the phrase "I don't know what went wrong," and feigning allergies at work in order to quell coworkers' questions about constant sniveling and puffy eyes. The best cure for PTBS is falling in love with someone new.

Sex with an ex can be depressing. If it's good you can't get it any more; if it's bad you just had sex with an ex.

—SAMANTHA,
SEX IN THE CITY

Purging

The emptying of all your ex's belongings from your habitat. Common methods include burning, boiling, eating, throwing, and defenestrating.

Rebounding

Throwing yourself at the first thing that moves after your breakup. Preferably, the moving thing is nonvehicular.

Schadenfreude

Finding joy in the fact that your ex has started to go to therapy three times a week since leaving you.

Soon-to-Be Ex

A boyfriend or girlfriend who is about to be single, regardless of whether or not he or she is aware of it. Yeah, we're talking about you.

Starter Marriage

A union formed when both parties are still in an emotionally zygotic state. It may or may not all be a ploy to procure a KitchenAid mixer and fondue set. The marriage won't last, but then again, most don't. The result is the starter divorce.

Wakaresaseya

Japanese firms that specialize in terminating relationships (see p. 19).

Wake-and-Ache

The moment when a new dumpee (or sometimes dumper) remembers several seconds after waking up alone in the morning that life is truly awful and might as well just be slept through. This might be true, but it's hard to make a living if you never exit the REM cycle. So get the hell up!

Web Stalking

Stalking your exes by Googling them every few minutes, calling them, opening their e-mail and/or mail, calling their friends, and/or checking their relationship status on Friendster or MySpace.

Breaking Down Breakup Styles

If she can't find me,

she can't break up with me.

—GEORGE COSTANZA, *SEINFELD*

Men are tricky. One day they're feeding you chocolate-covered strawberries in bed, and the next day they're complaining that you're too fat. And the ladies aren't immune to such tomfoolery. They claim they just want a nice guy, but then as soon as they find a nice guy, they decide they're bored.

If you are about to end a relationship, consider yourself lucky. After all, you're the dumper. You, dear reader, are the winner—you're the one who isn't about to face a cruel rejection.

So, the decision before you is what type of dump to choose. This isn't like selecting a spouse; this is important. You only get one chance.

And if you're on the other side and you're the one about to be sent packing, knowing the different types of breakups will help you identify one when it rolls your way ("Wait, are you trying the Slow Fade on me? Hello, I invented the Slow Fade!"). This will also help make it possible for you to end your relationship before your soon-to-be ex can, thus magically transforming a potential dumpee into a dumper, and the original dumper back into a frog.

So, for your convenience, we've outlined the most popular breakup methods for you, divided into a few basic categories.

Truth and Lies

The "It's Not Me, It's You"
Sometimes you don't just want to break up with your lover, you want to injure him or her emotionally. You want to make clear that you and only you want this relationship to end, and that the reason you want it to end is that he or she is a despicable human being. You want to walk out of this relationship with your head held high, knowing that you are single and free and that the other person will be forever left wondering if they were as bad in the sack as you say. In such a case, we suggest a novel technique that we believe will become a classic: The "It's Not Me, It's You." Prior to the breakup, you will want to come up with a laundry list of reasons that your significant other is disgusting. Do they go to the bathroom in the middle of the night and leave pee on the floor? Do they leave their tiny shaving hairs in the sink? It doesn't even matter if all the things you say are true. Just remember: this isn't about you, so don't let them change the subject. Your soon-to-be ex is the one that's filthy and disgusting, and, by the end of this breakup, he or she will know exactly why. If honesty is the best policy, then bring it on.

The "It's Not You, It's Me"
We include this popular breakup phrase only to beg that no one ever use it again. First off, it's clearly a blatant falsehood. What you are actually saying is, "It's not you, it's me, and my lack of attraction to you," which is the same as saying, "It's not me, it's you." Second, it makes you look like a buffoon to use such a cliché. Remember, the point of the

⟫⟩— **My First Breakup** ⟶

by Paula Froelich

First breakups are always the worst, especially when you have convinced yourself you are in love with the turd. I was in college, and it was the first guy I ever really fell in love with. We dated for three months during my summer break in Cincinnati. He was at the University of Cincinnati, I was at Emory. In retrospect, I should have known he was a jack-ass—he spent a year alone on top of a mountain "finding" himself, and anytime I would say something he didn't agree with he spent a lot of time telling me how superior he was because he had "found" himself. That and he had a creepy habit of befriending all of his other girlfriends' mothers and after every breakup would then stay friends with the mothers and not the women he had dated (hello, mother issues!). My mother loved him—he had redone our attic for free. She loved anyone who gave her something for free. So one night we went out and he was a real jerk, just not being very cool. Nasty comments, whatever, and I came home crying, and my mother, a tough Jewish lady from Queens who looks like Carla from *Cheers,* looked at me and said, "Get rid of him," before turning around and walking to the kitchen for some cheese (she likes cheese, though she is lactose intolerant). So, I did as my mother said and broke up with him.

The next day, he was shocked. A week later I asked him back, and he said no before hanging up the phone. I had never been rejected before and went a bit nutsy. I drove by his house five times a day for three weeks (until I gratefully went back to school in Atlanta). Called just to hear his voice (always hanging up—he later changed his number). And tried to seduce his best friend a week after he rejected me over a bottle of orange Mad Dog 20/20 (luckily it didn't work—the guy looked like Pee Wee Herman). True to form, a week after he said he didn't want me back, he called my mother "to talk." To her credit she told him to "talk to your own mother!" and hung up on him, later sniffing, "Like he thinks he can break MY daughter's heart and still talk to me? HA!" I eventually got over him and a year later saw him out. He was still as gorgeous as ever, but after five minutes of talking to him I couldn't believe I had ever been in love with such an insufferable ass. He propositioned me and I said, "Yeah, hmm, you know, I don't think so," and walked away. It felt great. Thankfully, I have never gotten so nutsy again, although once or twice I did take to bed for a day or two with a bottle of Jack and a carton of Marlboro Lights. But I never actually stalked anyone again.

> Paula Froelich is a reporter for the *New York Post* gossip column Page Six. She's also a correspondent on *The Insider* and author of the book *It! Nine Secrets of the Rich and Famous That Will Take You to the Top.*

---

breakup is often to make the other person feel bad while also absolving yourself of guilt. In the rare case that you actually still care about the other person and want them to leave the relationship unscathed, saying something as trite as "It's not you, it's me" will leave them feeling empty and cold and more alone than ever, and will make you feel guilty for lying.

The "I've Gotten Back Together with My Ex"
This is a favorite, especially among women. For some reason, suggesting that you're breaking up what is usually a new relationship because you want to rekindle things with someone you've already thrown to the curb makes a dumper feel a little less guilty, and the dumpee less bad. Perhaps this is because the dumper thinks the dumpee may feel that there is a possibility that one day in the future he or she will also get back together with this dumper, breaking up some future relationship. The dumper also thinks the dumpee may admire the perseverance it takes to make something work against all odds—even if that something is with someone else.

What's more, it's less threatening to tell a dumpee that you've been tempted by someone who preceded him or her than to say that you've simply lost interest or that he makes love like a frog trapped in a paper bag.

Unfortunately, it's nearly always a lie, as very few people actually break up with someone in order to get back with a former lover. But please, don't let the secret out.

The "Let's Get Married and Have a Million Babies"
Everybody wants someone to love them, until someone really, really loves them. Then it's just creepy. If you think

creepy love might scare off your significant other, you might want to combine obscene public displays of affection with conversations that begin with offhand comments like, "When we're married and have a million babies . . ." Be careful with this method, though. It can backfire, if in fact your significant other has severe self-esteem problems and reciprocates your creepy love . . . or if she's Mia Farrow. Then you might in fact get stuck with a million babies.

The "I'm Not Good Enough for You (and I'm Full of Crap)"

This breakup method comes highly recommended. While it is a transparent lie (if you weren't good enough, you'd be the one getting dumped), it is difficult to dispute. If done convincingly, the dumped party will experience a temporary rush of happiness even though you are dumping him or her. "Yah!" he or she will think. "I'm the better person!" It is only later, after you are dating someone more attractive, that the dumped party will recognize that he or she has been hoodwinked. Make sure that you have changed your phone number by then.

The "It's Just Not the Right Time"

"I like you, but it's just not the right time." We've all heard, and uttered, these dreadful words or a variation of them. They give us dumpees hope without actually giving us a relationship. Usually, it's a line that's spoken when one person is looking for more or less commitment than the other, but the truth is, if you're crazy enough about the person, you'll make right now be the right time.

Sometimes, the "right time" actually does come along. But most of the time, this line really means, "You're a seven, and I'm looking for like a nine. If I don't find a nine, and the eights are taken, I'll get back to you."

The "There's Someone Else"

This is a cruel but hilarious maneuver, especially when there isn't anyone else and you have to make up a whole fake biography for this Someone Else. It's a method that can sometimes help to deflect anger—especially if you name whom the nonexistent "someone else" is. It might be a good idea to make sure it's someone you don't like much, since there's a chance your soon-to-be ex will actually confront and interrogate the person you point to. Will it make you feel good to know that you've made yourself out to be a cheater? Maybe. It doesn't matter, though, because when the Someone Else tries to tell your ex that nothing ever happened, the Someone Else is the one who is going to look like a liar, and you'll walk away knowing that at least your ex thinks you were big enough to tell the truth.

Minimal-Effort Breakages

The "IM over You"

Too lazy to write a letter? Can't find a pen? Frightened that your significant other might jab a fork in your eye when you tell him or her that you've met someone else? This breakup technique might be for you. It's quick yet casual: just send your lover an instant message explaining why you're breaking it off, then quickly block them from your "buddy list." Better yet, change your screen name completely. In the Internet age, this is truly the most modern method of breaking up.

The "Slow Fade"

No, it's not a football play, it's an ancient breakup art involving the slow and gradual removal of one party (a.k.a. "you") from a relationship. Say that you talk to your future ex roughly ten times a week and shack up with him or her two evenings per week. Once the slow fade is put in motion, you will begin by cutting the phone calls from ten to eight. By the third week, you will cut the phone calls to six and visits to one and a half (you're there, but distant). This requires great patience, but within a few short months, you will simply be gone. Ideally, your lover won't even remember you were there.

The "Big Sleep"

This one works only if you have a lot of time on your hands, as it could interfere with occupational, familial, social, and monetary commitments. Otherwise, it's easy to pull off: all you need to do is sleep. Sleep all night, then, by golly, sleep all day! When you can sleep no longer, you'll just have to pretend. When your soon-to-be ex complains that you don't do anything but sleep anymore, play it off as a mysterious illness and drowsily blame the lack of a national health care system. Sickness is a hard one to argue with, but if he or she tries to fight you, it won't make much of a difference: you'll sleep through it.

The "Hit Man"

Not recommended.

Mind Games

The "I Can Tell You're Just Not That into This"

This tried and true breakup technique requires some acting skills, as it begins with a serious but entirely baseless conversation. Begin, if possible, by pretending to cry. Then, announce that you've figured out that your soon-to-be ex doesn't seem to be as into the relationship as you are. (You might need ammunition, so try preparing a few days in advance. Did he or she make a cup of coffee and not make you one too? Did he or she not treat last time you went out to dinner? Is the sex lasting too long, showing that your lover is not turned on by you as much as he used to be? Present these facts.) Say you're disappointed he doesn't seem to want to make things work out. If he says, "What are you talking about?" just use it against him. "You see? You don't even realize how you've been pushing me away. You're not even aware of my existence."

The "Houdini"

Have you cheated on and lied to your loved one? It may not be wise for you to linger; it might be smart for you to simply . . . disappear. The Houdini is the simplest trick in the breakup book (no mess!), yet surprisingly difficult to pull off. The key to executing the Houdini is to avoid going to the places your ex frequents, and not to leave items at your ex's place that you may need. You also may want to change your phone numbers, and write "return to sender" on any mail you might receive from your soon-to-be ex. Of course, there are people who've ended up on the six o'clock news using this method and have made the government use taxpayer dollars to find them—but if that's the price to be paid to be free, so be it.

The "Lucy Van Pelt"

So you're in a relationship with someone for whom you care deeply, but you don't want to commit, because you're too young, or because it's not fun sleeping with just one person (without anyone else watching). In such a situation, the Lucy Van Pelt may be for you. Lucy, you might recall, is the Peanuts character who is always holding out the football for Charlie Brown, then yanking it away at the last moment, thus confusing poor Charlie (who, good soul that he is, will keep trying to kick the football). The Lucy Van Pelt constitutes sending constant mixed messages (like booty calls but no next-morning calls) that will keep your relationship on the rocks without fully ending it. It's a breakup method oft employed by femmes fatales, although men have been known to it use it as well, especially when juggling multiple women. Eventually, you will have to take the football away completely, or let him kick it. But, in the meantime, you can have the best sex of your life while figuring out whether you're ready to settle down. This can also be a cruel but fun way to play with the mind of someone you don't like very much.

The "Break Up or Get Married"

At the end of a relationship, there's a sentence that gets blurted out with alarming frequency: "Either we need to break up or get married." It usually comes out mid-argument. But don't be fooled. It's always a ploy. If someone really wants to marry you, they're not going to ask you in ultimatum form. So what's the advantage of this type of breakup? It buys time, while the soon-to-be ex weighs the age-old question about marriage and breakups: which is the lesser evil?

Movie Star Splits

The "Hugh Grant" (a.k.a. the "Jude Law")
If you're dating someone truly fabulous, like, say, Elizabeth Hurley or Sienna Miller, but still want to end the relationship, you're going to have to do something really dramatic. In such an instance, sleeping with someone below your social rank may be the ideal solution. Try a babysitter, or a hooker. Or perhaps you know a babysitter who also hooks. Of course, this must be planned carefully, since you not only must find and court a babysitter-cum-hooker but also must get caught in the act. This should end things pretty quickly, and will also get you a lot of attention from your friends (and possibly the media). The downside of the "Hugh Grant" is, if you're not a successful film and television actor, your employer may frown on such behavior, and you might be left without child care.

The "Anne Heche"
The most difficult part of a breakup can be remaining friends. If that's what you're after, sample the "Anne Heche." It's simple: tell your lover, "You're great, but I'm not attracted to . . . your gender anymore." Since the person you're trying to lose isn't the problem—it's just his

genitals!—it's more likely your soon-to-be ex will say that it's okay if you're gay, or straight, or whatever, and will want to remain friends through this confusing process. The "Anne Heche" can also be used to refer to breakups in which you tell your partner, "It's not you, it's . . . these crazy voices in my head."

The "Billy Crudup"
This one is a male classic, in that it's worked for centuries and is the reason so many of us are distant cousins: men like to sleep with more than one woman and then blame the male genetic makeup—not themselves. Sometimes, however, he realizes this only once he has already knocked up woman (or wife) number one.

Sure, you could save face and suffer through a few years of changing diapers. But you could also find a younger lady to sidle up against (why not Claire Danes?) and let the first one fend for herself. This will not endear you to her. But if you're the exquisite but confused Mary Louise Parker, you might just name the spawn after Daddy anyway.

The "Brad Pitt"
Your significant other is hot, wealthy, and glamorous . . . but wait, so are you! What else could you possibly want in life? You want to make tiny Brads to follow in your giant footsteps. Unfortunately, the lady in your life does not, so you take matters into your own hands and find someone who is even hotter and happens to love babies, even ones that aren't her own. The trick with this one is to confuse everyone around you—including your ex—by continually

professing your love for the one you're about to leave, and by picking a new mating partner who looks like she's actually more interested in eating children than birthing them.

The "Britney Spears" (a.k.a. the "Nicky Hilton")
So you're incredibly wealthy white trash, and you need to shake off that annoying lover. Oh, do we have an unconventional breakup method for you: marry the loser! Ideally, this should happen in Las Vegas, and you should wear a trucker hat during the ceremony. After a night of having raucous, unsafe sex—what the hey, you're married!—announce to your soon-to-be ex that you must get an annulment because your people don't approve of you marrying while sloshed: "My publicist says we should just be friends." After the annulment, you'll never see that deadbeat again—and you'll be free to find another trashy thing to marry.

> You can't stay married in a situation
> where you are afraid to go to sleep
> in case your wife might cut your throat.
> —MIKE TYSON

PROFILES IN NOT-A-LOT-OF-COURAGE

Elizabeth Taylor

Elizabeth Taylor is one of the few women in the world who can say she got divorced at least once a decade from 1950 to 2000. The eight-time-married septuagenarian picked a wide array of men to love and leave and lose.

Here's an inventory:

Husband 1: Nicky Hilton, May 1950–January 1951
> He was a hotel heir. Also Zsa Zsa Gabor's stepson and Paris Hilton's great-uncle. Liz divorced him, claiming physical abuse.

Husband 2: Michael Wilding, February 1952–January 1957
> He was an actor, and Liz was the second of his four wives. They had two sons together.

Husband 3: Mike Todd, February 1957–March 1958
> Born Avrom Hirsch Goldbogen, Todd was an acclaimed film producer, and he and Liz had a daughter. But Liz was then widowed when he died in a plane crash shortly thereafter.

Husband 4: Eddie Fisher, May 1959–March 1964
> He'd been Mike Todd's best friend, but when Todd died Fisher divorced his wife, Debbie Reynolds, so he could get together with Liz. She converted to Judaism for him, and remained Jewish after the divorce.

Husband 5: Richard Burton, March 1964–June 1974
> They met on the set of *Cleopatra*. She renounced her U.S. citizenship for him. They starred in *Who's Afraid of Virginia Woolf?* in which they played parts similar to whom they were offscreen: married, arguing alcoholics.

Husband 6: Richard Burton, October 1975–July 1976
> Again!

Husband 7: John Warner, December 1976–November 1982
> A Virginia senator with really bad hair.

Husband 8: Larry Fortensky, October 1991–October 1996
> He was a construction worker who hadn't even been born at the time of Liz's first marriage. They met in rehab, and were married at Michael Jackson's home.

Fifty Ways to Get Your Lover
to Leave You

What's that? You've tried to leave your lover and it's just not working? You've tried to slip out the back, Jack, and make a new plan, Stan, yet you come home and she's still there?

Paul Simon's famous song suggested fifty ways to leave your lover, but sometimes leaving your lover isn't going to do the trick. Instead, you need to get your lover to leave you. That way, he or she will look like a commitment-phobic cretin to all your friends and you might get a better divorce settlement.

So, here's our quickie guide to fifty little ways to get someone to quickly despise you:

1) become a hard-core NASCAR fan
2) take up chain-smoking
3) stop bathing
4) leave different-colored hairs on your pillow
5) tell your soon-to-be ex that you have a secret: you are a schizophrenic, and the person he or she has been dating is actually your alter ego, while the true you is Rosalita, a Mexican drag queen who enjoys salsa dancing and meeting strangers in the bathrooms of dark bars
6) tell your soon-to-be ex you have a rare sexually transmitted disease that had previously been found only in the jungles of Ecuador
7) convert to an exotic religion and then insist that everything your lover is doing constitutes religious discrimination
8) start all sentences with, "You know who is really hot . . ."

9) garlic

10) threesomes

11) foursomes

12) get a pet that your soon-to-be ex is allergic to, preferably a bunny

13) buy your soon-to-be ex a pager, then insist that he or she check in every hour

14) leave the door open when you're in the bathroom

15) remove the door from your bathroom

16) shave with an electric razor, then leave all the tiny hairs in the sink

17) wear headphones at all times; when your soon-to-be ex talks to you, lip-synch along to a song

18) insert the word *literally* into every sentence

19) download copious amounts of pornography on your shared computer

20) insist on a carb-free, sugar-free, and gluten-free home

21) watch the *Rocky Horror Picture Show* on DVD nightly

22) revert to baby talk at all times

23) put your name on all items in the fridge that you purchased

24) get a mullet

25) inquire as to what shampoo your soon-to-be ex uses to make their hair so greasy

26) spandex

27) set your watch ahead an hour, and constantly complain about everyone else's tardiness

28) snore

29) start keeping books about bestiality on your coffee table

30) program your Tivo to record all episodes of *The Blue Collar Comedy Hour*

31) eat shoots and leaves

32) convince your soon-to-be ex to let you gamble his or her money

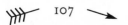

33) renounce materialism and give up all your possessions

34) whenever your soon-to-be ex asks you to do something, like take out the trash, quote Bart Simpson: "I can't promise to try, but I'll try to try"

35) gain forty pounds, buy skimpier clothes

36) make up cutesy nicknames for everything

37) insist on public displays of affection

38) ladies, stop shaving your legs; men, start shaving your chest

39) announce you will soon be starring in a movie with Angelina Jolie

40) sign up for an online dating service using your soon-to-be ex's credit card

41) insist that all household decisions be made by a roll of the dice

42) run up huge phone bills voting for your favorite *American Idol* contestant

43) never offer to pay for anything

44) stop cutting your pinkie nail

45) chew the ends of all the pens in the house

46) stop doing dishes and then start putting the dirty plates and pots in the refrigerator, assuring your soon-to-be ex that this will keep away the roaches

47) stop taking your meds

48) talk about how, if you ever break up, the thing you'll miss most about your soon-to-be ex is his or her wireless access

49) start using the "royal we"

50) give this book as a gift

I've had three lovers in the past four years,
and they all ran a distant second to a good book and a warm bath.

—DOROTHY BOYD, *JERRY MAGUIRE*

BREAKUP CUSTOMS

Malaysia: The Beetlejuice Divorce Plan

Under Islamic law still in effect in certain countries, a husband can divorce his wife by repeating the phrase "I divorce you" three times. However, he better not do it without thinking first—he can't marry her again until the woman marries someone else who then chooses to divorce her.

In the end, the whole thing can be done faster than you can say, well, "I divorce you."

Recently, the government of Malaysia decreed that this Beetlejuice approach to divorce need not be done in person; an e-mail, instant message, or even a text message will suffice. No word yet on whether couples counseling will soon be available via text message, too.

Lost in Translation:
What Men and Women Really Mean
When They're Breaking Up with You

And just so you know, it's not that common,
it doesn't happen to every guy, and it is a big deal.
—RACHEL GREEN, *FRIENDS*

Breakups, like relationships, are packed with lies.

Although we strongly support lying when we're dumping someone, we have come to hate these very same lies when we're the ones being jilted, because they can cause us years of unnecessary confusion as we play the lines over and over in our minds.

Believing common untruths like "It's Not You, It's Me" can cost you great misery. Did he really love me and it just wasn't the right time? Should I wait for him so when it is the right time we can be together?

Fortunately, most dumpers aren't all that creative, so they resort to the standard clichés (read: lies!) that will end things more quickly. For your breakup ease, we've created a little guide to help you figure out what he or she really meant when the following lines were uttered.

THE LINE	SHE MEANS	HE MEANS
"It's not you, it's me."	You're way more into this than I am.	I'm looking for a nine, and you're a seven.
"I love you, but I'm just not 'in love' with you."	You bore me, although I guess you'd do if there were no other options out there.	When we're having sex, I pretend you're someone else.
"We can still be friends."	Could you still maybe install my air conditioner for me?	If you want, I'll still bang you from time to time.
"This is just too much for me right now."	Coddling your ego has worn me out.	You're cutting into my porn time.
"I know one day I'll regret this."	I'm trying to make you feel better by making up something ridiculous.	Now that I've said something meaningful, can I go play beer pong?
"I'm just not attracted to you anymore."	Actually, I was never really attracted to you, but I thought I'd give it a shot because in the movies it always works when the cute girl dates the ugly duckling.	You were attractive to me only when you were unattainable. However, now that I've got you, I find you revolting.
"I'm too young to settle down."	I'm only twelve!	I'm only forty!

THE LINE	SHE MEANS	HE MEANS
"You deserve someone better than me."	I deserve someone better than you.	If you put out more, I think we could probably work this out.
"We have different goals."	I'd like to find a meaningful relationship with a man who under-stands and adores me, and I don't think this is you.	I aspire to watch every episode of *Scooby Doo* in one sitting.

The Perfect Breakup Medium for You

Why do you have to break up with her?

Be a man! Just stop calling!

—JOEY TRIBBIANI, *FRIENDS*

If you're a decent human being, there is only one way to break up with someone: in person. Yes, that's right: you're going to have to see your soon-to-be ex one last time if you want to fully extricate yourself from your failed relationship.

But many of you are not so decent, especially those of you who have penises. So, in case you simply cannot bear breaking up with your soon-to-be ex in person, or in case you fear that an in-person breakup will prevent any breakup and lead to sex (the horror!), we are going to try to help you explore some alternative mediums.

So You Want to Break Up by . . . Instant Messenger

When It's Appropriate
The IM is a painfully easy—and lazy—way to break up with someone, and we suggest it be used only for relationships that have lasted fewer than two weeks and have been generally dispassionate and casual. There's a good chance, however, that your soon-to-be ex has perceived your union as more serious than you have, and will not appreciate being dumped by an emoticon. : (

What's Good about It
It's quick and fast, and you can multitask while doing it. You get all the immediacy of an actual in-person conversation, but you don't have to watch the other person suffer (you can watch TV while she's suffering). This actually can be a bonus for the dumpee too, as he or she can play it cool—heartbreak hides well behind a keyboard.

What's Bad about It
IMs don't have the ephemeral and private qualities that other methods do. Every sentence can be easily cut and pasted into someone else's IM window, which means that your soon-to-be ex might be sharing your breakup lines in real time with another IMer. What's more, people usually don't think out what they type in IMs with the same care they do when writing e-mails or letters, yet an IM can be saved just as simply. Do you want your ex using those words against you when you come back after realizing there's

nothing better out there? And do you ever want your breakup to include the phrase "LOL"?

Things to Keep in Mind
Tone is something that's difficult to convey in an instant message—a statement that's meant to come across as ironic can easily be misconstrued as heartfelt, and vice versa. This is an issue that some people try to solve by using emoticons, but admit it: the only thing more pathetic than using instant messenger to breakup with someone is using a colon and a parenthesis to convey feelings of remorse.

So You Want to Break Up . . .
over the Phone

When It's Appropriate
If you're dating long distance and need to do the deed before you're going to see your soon-to-be ex in person, the phone might be the way to go. It's also understandable to want to break up on the phone if you've gone on a few dates with someone, or had sexual relations with him after one or twelve beers, but never had any intention of actually being in a relationship. Intention is critical here. If you never felt emotionally involved, if this was always just a fling, feel free to dial away.

What's Good about It
Sometimes it's easier to say things over the phone that you can't say in person but need to say in order to make the

HINTS

Anna Jane Says:
Take Pride in Knowing How to Take a Hint

If there's one thing that makes people cowardly, it's dating. Say you've been out with someone once or twice. Say you liked the person just fine, but you also wouldn't really care if you never saw him again. What's the easiest way to convey this feeling of apathy? Don't do anything!

Yes, it's the most pathetic approach. But, if a good hinter encounters a good hint taker, it can be the most painless breakup method possible.

So how do you know if someone is trying to give you a hint?

The person will stop calling, will stop returning calls, will cancel dates, and will not return e-mails. No, he is not playing hard to get. He wasn't run over by a truck. He hasn't stopped checking his e-mail. He hasn't lost your number. He hasn't been planning you a surprise party.

He's just not interested.

So cry into your pillow, complain to your best friend about the injustice of it all, announce you'll never date again, and then . . .

Move on to the next.

Or, if you feel you really must have the last word, e-mail the hint giver telling him simply that you get that you've been shown the door.

breakup final. And, when someone is crying over the phone, it's not as sad. Plus, if it goes on too long, you can hang up and blame it on a bad connection.

Also, there's the possibility of phone sex . . .

HINTS

Flint Says:
Take Pride in Knowing How Not to Take a Hint

Hmmm, sounds suspiciously like that "he's just not that into you" claptrap. Obviously, lovely Anna Jane and the authors of that other book have the germ of a point. They are right in arguing that if you think someone is trying to give you a hint, they probably are.

But here's where I part ways with them: I believe that some of the greatest relationships are the result of persistence. Two out of three of my serious relationships began with me being rejected . . . repeatedly. If I had accepted their hints, I would have never spoken to them again. Instead, I hung around, not like a stalker but like a young slugger who is willing to put in a few years in double-A ball to get his shot at the big leagues.

Love doesn't always happen overnight. Sometimes, great love requires great obstacles, and one of those obstacles can be that the other person doesn't like you all that much, or likes you just as a friend . . . at first. So, hear the hints, know the hints, and don't keep trying to hump a leg that doesn't want to be humped. But don't run away either. If you like someone, stick around and fight for them. John Cusack would have.

What's Bad about It
Besides the fact that it's morally repugnant, absolutely nothing.

Things to Keep in Mind
The person on the other end of the line can tell if you're not paying attention, and can hear if you're typing

e-mails to your new love interest. The bigger issue is that if you care about someone enough to have a conversation with her or him about your breakup, you should care enough to be doing it in person. Even more important, you never know who is listening, like her mother, or the government.

So You Want to Break Up . . . in a Letter

When It's Appropriate

It's pretty much always appropriate to break up in a letter if the relationship was a meaningful one. At the same time, it's always inappropriate to break up using a postcard with a picture of a hot woman or man on the beach under the sentence, "Wish you were here (not)."

What's Good about It

A letter allows your thoughts time to breathe, and it lets you explain without interruption. The recipient can read it over and over again and really process the reason you are ending things. If well written, it will be something the recipient may eventually cherish. You can also use it as an opportunity to practice your cursive.

What's Bad about It

Most people in the modern world can barely string a sentence together. If you can't spell *breakup* without spell-check then, well, you better make sure to use spell-check. Otherwise, stick to the phone. Keep in mind that a breakup letter should be poetic, not a string of clichés. If you're not going to be able to do it right, don't do it at all. Also, there's the difficulty of deciding how to sign off. You can't do "Sincerely" or "All my best," but you also can't do "All my love" or "Forever yours."

Things to Keep in Mind

Sometimes someone will draft a breakup letter with the original intention of using the letter as a reference during an actual in-person breakup, but then it starts to seem like it would be easier to just mail the "notes" or hand them to the soon-to-be ex. This isn't recommended. If you're going to take the trouble to write a letter, make it as elegant as you can—no one wants to receive a stack of three-by-five-inch index cards with the alphabetically categorized reasons they're getting dumped. When breaking up via letter, it's ideal not to mail the letter since you never know if it could get lost, but to leave it where the recipient can't miss it, and to make sure your soon-to-be ex knows you're available for an in-person chat after he or she has taken a few days to think about and/or burn the letter.

So You Want to Break Up . . . by E-mail

When It's Appropriate

If you draft your e-mail like an actual letter, you can use it as you would use a paper letter. However, if you're going to just dash off a note without regard to, say, capital letters, a breakup e-mail should be reserved for more casual relationships—specifically ones where the person won't leave you alone.

What's Good about It

E-mail breakups have many of the qualities of an actual breakup letter, except a) you don't have to worry about it getting lost in the mail, b) it's in a good format if you want to forward it to friends to get their opinion before you send it, and c) it's easy to have a copy of it to look back at and re-gret later. But the best use of the breakup e-mail is for a re-lationship where, despite other efforts, the soon-to-be ex isn't getting the message that you're no longer interested. This is usually someone with whom you've been out only a few times and he or she insists on calling you incessantly even when you never return the calls. A letter would be too precious; a phone call would involve having to call him or her back. An e-mail is the perfect compromise.

What's Bad about It

When a breakup e-mail is heartfelt, there's a risk of it com-ing off as being too casual. The e-mail format also deprives your soon-to-be ex of the dramatic postreading ripping apart of the breakup letter. And, if sitcoms are to be be-lieved, you could accidentally send it to everyone you know.

Things to Keep in Mind

If this is an e-mail going to someone who won't leave you alone, make sure to be as clear and concise as possible. There's no point in waxing profuse—it'll only give the poor sap a false sense of hope.

Try something like this:

Dear [Name],

I'm flattered by your pursuance of me. However, while I enjoyed our dates, I'm currently [busy seeing someone new/putting a lot of energy into making a rubber-band ball] and that's really taking up all my attention and time.

You are [kind/a little creepy], and I hope you'll understand that I cannot reciprocate any feelings you have for me.

It would be easiest if you didn't call, ever.

I'm sorry. Good luck in your career as a [lawyer/ dentist/stalker/stunt clown].

[Name]

(EDITOR'S NOTE: This is based on an e-mail Anna Jane actually sent to a pesky suitor. It didn't work—he continued to call. But this was clearly an extenuating circumstance, as Anna Jane is unusually irresistible to losers.)

So You Want to Break Up . . . through a Friend

When It's Appropriate
Having a friend break up for you is really only appropriate if you're in junior high, or if you're in a body cast.

What's Good about It
What isn't good about it?! You get spared the agony of having to figure out what to say, and your ex gets

I haven't missed you. In fact, I've been revoltingly unfaithful to you.
—DOLORES "LOLITA" HAZE,
LOLITA

someone to comfort them—someone who is rejecting them only by proxy. Also, your friend might get lucky.

What's Bad about It
You get no knowledge of what really went on during the breakup. But, obviously, you don't care.

Things to Keep in Mind
You're an asshole.

The Breakup Pocket Guide

You know when you're at the blackjack table and you're sitting on fifteen and the dealer is showing a king and you're like, "Man, I wish I had a quickie pocket guide to know what to do in this situation"?

Well, we don't have that guide, but we do have a quickie (mmmm, quickie) pocket guide for when you're about to break up but don't know whether you have to do it in person or can just disappear gently into the dark night, and the arms of a stranger . . .

KEY	
Ignore, ignore, ignore	0
IM or text message	1
Write an e-mail	2
Call	3
Suck it up and do it in person	4
Write a letter	5
Get someone else to do it for you	6
Publicly humiliate	7
Try to fix the person up with someone else	8
The person and/or situation probably isn't worth the trouble, so do nothing	9

THE BREAKUP POCKET GUIDE
IF YOU WANT TO . . .

The status and the reason you want to break up:	stay friends	possibly reunite at some point	ruin his/her life (or at least his/her week)	sever all ties
One or two dates, no physical contact, and you . . .				
just don't like the person	Why would you be friends with someone you don't like?	1 or 2	9	0
have no chemistry	1–4, or 9	If there's no chemistry now, there probably won't be any later.	9	0
One or two dates, fooling around, and you . . .				
just don't like the person	People you don't like make lousy friends, unless they're friends with benefits	2, followed up by a possible booty call	7	0 or 4 (and tell the truth)
have religious or political differences	2–4, and avoid reading the *Nation* or *Weekly Standard* together	2–4, and consider converting	9 (it's a free country)	0 or 7
have no chemistry	2–4	2–4	9	0
Three to four dates and you . . .				
are commitment-phobic	2–5, and make it heartfelt	2 or 3	Be more concerned they'll want to ruin your life.	6
met someone better	4 (but you might want to fudge the truth)	You're a jerk.	You're a jerk.	You're a jerk.

The status and the reason you want to break up:	stay friends	possibly reunite at some point	ruin his/her life (or at least his/her week)	sever all ties
Five to ten dates and . . .				
you are commitment-phobic	Can you really commit to a friendship?	2–5	0	8 (but make sure it's someone who'll bad-mouth you)
you cheated	Good luck!	You must be Flint.	1 (and tell the whole truth)	6 (preferably the person you cheated with)
met someone better	4 (but don't mention your new conquest)	4 (but lie)	4 (and use the phrase "I've met someone better")	0
the other person cheated	Get a spine.	You're a wimp.	7	0
More than twenty dates and . . .				
you are commitment-phobic	4 (and lie or tell the truth at your own discretion)	4 (and lie or tell the truth at your own discretion)	0	4 (tell the truth, and say you'll never change)
you cheated	4 (and lie)	Send mixed messages.	4 (and bring the newbie with you)	0
you are just not in love	4 (and lie or tell the truth at your own discretion)	8	3 (and tell the truth)	4 (tell the truth and say, "I want to sever all ties")
the other person cheated	7, just to get even. Then a friendship may be able to be built.	0	4	1

))))— A Breakup Letter That Backfired ⟶

In June 2003, Paul Kelly Tripplehorn Jr., an intern in a senator's office in Washington, D.C., banged out this angry missive to a girl he was trying to lose.

However, when his dumpee received the e-mail, she cleverly forwarded it to everyone she knew, and it wasn't long before it got leaked to the tabloids.

Although Tripplehorn threatened to have the girl blackballed, in the end he's the one who lost his job because of the breakup.

From: Kelly Tripplehorn
Sent: Tuesday, June 03, 2003 2:11 PM
Subject: you suck

Well, as of this afternoon, I was planning on ruining your career by making phone calls to all of my parents friends and have you blackballed from the workplace as well as every prestigious law school in the country, but then (lucky for you) I decided not to do that because you are a sad sad person and I will just let your life self destruct right before my eyes.

Michele I am sorry, I don't care how big of a sadistic fucked up crush you have on me but people like me simply don't date people like you. You are too competitive with me and you just simply will never be better than me. I will always have more friends than you just because I don't care about beating people and lying to get to the top. (You are

(continues)

---

an absolute hypocrite in everything that you do, I am not going to go into details why you are because that would be a waste of my time and yours but I can assure you if you were to ever meet yourself you would hate your twin) I have told most all of the staff about our situation now and they already knew you were really messed up. They said when you were talking to them about me, they all told me you had 'serious issues' and that every word you said sounded scripted and they knew without a doubt that you were lying. I have noticed that people who you think are your good friends actually really dislike you but unlike me, they will not tell you to your face because they would rather be fake nice to you than be your enemy.

Now talking about how I am obsessed with money, I simply am not. You are. You always are trying to impress me by how much money you have and I don't care. The difference is though I talk about it but it is never about bragging and it is never directly about money, it is always directly about the conversation. For instance, someone will ask, what are you doing for July 4th? And then I will say I am going to Aspen. It is a simple fact that I am but since you don't have a house in Aspen, you get offended because of your competitive nature. When you talk about money you will say something like [University of Texas'] tuition is 5% of your family's income, thus my tuition would be 125,000. Yea, Michele you are right, I brag too much about what I have.

Well I am just going to stop writing because you are just absolutely beneath me. I have heard that you try to undermine people all the time that are better than you and every single time it does not work because people can see through such shallowness and that is why as I have heard so many times, most "everyone at UT absolutely hates you." For instance even the people that you thought were your friends . . . they hate you, they just never say anything. Everyone knows you are a pathetic social climber who will go to any disgusting means to move up the ladder. But guess what Michele, you will never move up the ladder because I am at the top and people like me hate people like you. You might be able to trick people like me for maybe a month or so but your true personality comes through after a while and it is vile, if that. You have sooooo many people that absolutely hate you and you will never know it because they will never say anything to your face. You will not succeed in life and even the staff thinks that also, after I told them about the things that you do. You suck and good luck being miserable for the rest of your life. I do not even know why I wasted my time typing this for suck slime. Everyone tells me that you are so beneath me (which you are) and I should not get worked up over suck trifles. By the end of the day if I wanted to, I could make a phone call and have your life absolutely ruined but there is no need because you are falling fast enough towards failure without me. In the end, all I can say is that people love me and people hate you. You should observe me and take a few notes on how to make real friends. Other than you tying this one other person, I have never had such little respect for a human being

(continues)

in my life. I don't even have to tell you why because in my very accurate analysis that most everyone else agrees with, if you were to agree with my analysis about your character then my whole entire analysis would be wrong. Your inflamed ego has left you so blind and so impotent that you can not even recognize the most obvious flaws in yourself. All your old roommates absolutely hated you and you still think the problem is with them, not you. Well I talked to your roommates and I thought they nice normal girls. So naturally, you would not fit in with them because you are so intellectually above them all. Right? You suck at life and you need to figure out why or you will be miserable for the rest of your life.

Once again from your intellectual, moral, social, and emotional superior,

Paul Kelly Tripplehorn Jr.

It's Mine! It's All Mine!
A Guide to Splitting Up
the Postbreakup Booty

I'm an excellent housekeeper.
Every time I get a divorce, I keep the house.
—ZSA ZSA GABOR

Splitting up things that have exchanged hands during a relationship is a tricky business. (That's why lawyers are so good at it.)

But why hire a sharky attorney when you can peruse our guide to getting what's rightfully yours?

First, a word of advice: the best thing to do is to give your ex everything that you can reasonably part with. Graciousness is a rare quality in a breakup, but it's one we advocate, in theory. If you are the dumper and have decided that you'd now like to get with your ex's best friend, being very generous might help you get over those pesky guilty feelings. On the other hand, if you're the dumpee, you might be hoping that your ex is feeling majorly guilty. So you'll want to play up your victimhood by dramatically relinquishing all possessions accumulated during the relationship.

And then there are situations where you just want to get your crap back and don't want to waste time with mind games. If that's the place you're in, read on.

If You're Not Living Together

In cases of noncohabitation, you should assume anything your ex has left at your home is yours. His favorite T-shirt, the one that smells like college? Yours if you want it. Feel free to wear it or to make it into a rag. That bottle of Valium? Pop away! His or her wallet? Finders keepers (American Express weepers!). Anything you don't want and don't feel like returning can always be sold on eBay or Craig's List.

There's a chance, however, that he or she might bug you about wanting stuff back. Should this be the case, we have three words for you: *avoid, avoid, avoid.* Phone numbers can be changed. E-mails can, too, even identities. Did you always want to be a blonde? Now is the time. And you can always put a new name on your doorbell to cause confusion should he or she come by in person.

Or, you can make appointments to drop things off and then cancel at the last minute. Eventually, your ex will get fed up and just buy a new toothbrush (a healthy habit regardless of your dating situation).

To make sure you don't end up on the other side of this equation, we suggest never leaving anything at anyone's home if it's something you are not ready to give up.

However, if you have made the mistake of leaving a special pair of undies at your ex's and you are now determined to get them back, we have another three words to impart, because you are despicably cheap: *pester, pester, pester.*

Call, drop by, and then call again. Write a letter if you need to, and don't be afraid to get a cop to do some of the pestering for you. If you can't convince a cop to get on your side, you can always pay a stripper to dress up like one.

If You Are Living Together

Once spaces and belongings have been combined, things get complicated.

If you can still tolerate one another, the distribution can go rather smoothly; however, just because you can't be in the same room without being armed with mace doesn't mean possessions can't be equitably divided.

But first, remember: anything that you brought into the relationship should be yours when you leave, period.

Don't be afraid to write your name in the books and on the pans that were yours before you found yourself sharing a studio apartment that would normally not be big enough for an Oompa-Loompa. Don't be ashamed—think of it as a poor man's prenuptial agreement.

Things that were purchased jointly, or during those dark years of coupledom, are a different story.

Here are our thoughts on how things should be split up:

	If you're getting along . . .	If you hate each other . . .
Books	Books purchased during the relationship should be divvied at the discretion of the person who actually laid out the cash for the book. If there was no clear purchaser or if, say, *The*	Either abscond with all the books you can while your ex is sleeping, or leave all the books with your ex but take his or her library card and then go borrow the 388 books you left from the library and have them all go

	If you're getting along . . .	If you hate each other . . .
	Unbearable Lightness of Being was given to you as a joint gift and you both want it, then you either need to sell it secondhand and split the money, or buy another copy as cheaply as possible. Try looking at http://www.isbn.nu. If this method doesn't appeal, try putting all the contested books in a bag and take turns fishing them out grab-bag style. Books on tape should be exploded with dynamite, regardless of who purchased them.	under his or her account (those nickel charges add up fast). Books on tape should be exploded with dynamite, regardless of who purchased them.
Music	CDs can be easily copied or made into MP3s, so if you devote a few hours to it, you and your ex can walk away from the relationship with the same music library for the cost of as many blank CDs. Don't have the time? Get an intern to do it for you at work. That's what they're there for.	Furtively take all the CDs you want, but leave the jewel cases on the shelf.
Wedding Jewelry	Splitting jewelry can sometimes be a legal matter. That's right—there are breakup laws! In most states, a wedding ring belongs to whoever is—er, was—wearing it. The engagement ring traditionally is considered the property of the woman since it was given to her as a gift, so it's up to her whether to keep it or return it . . . or to sell it.	Sue for all the bling. Even if your ex says you can have the ring or rings, sue anyway. Nothing says "I loathe you" more than dragging someone needlessly into a lawsuit. Remember, there are a lot of lawyers out there who need to feed their children.

	If you're getting along . . .	If you hate each other . . .
	Usually, she doesn't return it unless it was an heirloom in the man's family.	
Pets	Usually one person has a slightly closer bond to an animal than the other person, or else one person has a schedule that's more accommodating to pets. This is the person that should get the pets, but the ex should be allowed to visit or borrow the animal if he or she wants to get on *Stupid Pet Tricks.* If this fails, there's always cloning.	Take the pet, and replace it with one that looks similar. Then let hilarity ensue.
Furniture	Draw up a list of all the pieces of furniture that need to be divided, then discuss which one of you wants or needs each piece more. Try to split things in such a way that you both feel you've gotten some things that were really important to you. If one person is going to get the bulk of the furniture, he or she should offer to drive the other person to Ikea, and should offer to contribute to the cost of new items.	Tell your ex you have been unfaithful, and then get specific: you were unfaithful on the bed, on the sofa, and on the kitchen table. If your ex insists on taking the furniture anyway, try mentioning that the person you slept with on the sofa, table, and bed had really bad lice.
Photos	Digital photos can be copied onto disks so that each person has them. Nondigital photos can be copied also if you have the negatives. If you don't, take them to where they can scan them onto a disk. If the photos are indecent, this latter method might net you a new	Steal the photos, then digitally remove your ex (assuming you look hot in the pictures) and replace him or her with a supermodel.

	If you're getting along . . .	**If you hate each other . . .**
	lover, depending on how you look naked and whether you're into dating people who work at Kinko's.	
Dishes	Whoever picked out the pattern should get to keep the dishes, but he or she should then help select and pay for the ex's new set.	Supposedly, Beethoven used to throw dishes when he was angry. You too can be like Beethoven.
Friends	Friends usually divide on their own. If they don't, they should be able to split time between both of you.	Do whatever it takes—including spreading vicious lies—to win over your ex's friends and make your ex end up with no one to call but you.

Places	If you share a favorite restaurant or video store that you are both going to want to continue to frequent after the breakup, you might worry about having to be there at the same time (especially if you're on a date). If this is the case, one of you should be allowed to go to it for the first six months of every year, and the other should have access for the second six months. Or you can each take it for one-half of every week.	Go to all your favorite haunts and tell them that your ex is a shoplifter.
		
		    Offer a photo that they can tape next to the register so that the person on duty knows to keep an eye out.
		
		    While you're at it, bring your own photo and tell all the restaurant owners that you are a food critic.

Do me a favor, for your own good, put your name in your books

right now before they get mixed up and you won't know whose is whose.

'Cause someday, believe it or not, you'll go fifteen rounds

over who's gonna get this coffee table.

This stupid, wagon-wheel, Roy Rogers, garage-sale coffee table.

—HARRY, *WHEN HARRY MET SALLY*

How to Use Points to Divide Things

This is a simplified version of the "Adjusted Winner" algorithm. No, we don't know what an algorithm is either, but it sounds pretty fancy, eh? (We didn't make it up—it was developed by Steven J. Brams and Alan D. Taylor, authors of the book *The Win-Win Solution*.)

Step 1: Make two identical lists of all the things you are trying to split up—do not include items that can't be easily sold, like friends or pets. Unless you operate in the black market, you shouldn't include children.

Let's say your items are a particle-board Ikea bookshelf, an *Elton John Greatest Hits, 1970–2002* CD, a cordless drill, and an economy-size package of ramen noodles.

Step 2: You and your ex both write on your respective lists a point value that corresponds to how much you want the possession. Your points, when added up, must equal one hundred.

So, imagine you have allotted the ramen noodles fifty-five points, because it's the only thing you know how to cook. The drill, you give ten points. You're not a *Tool Time* type. You then give the bookshelf thirty points, and the Elton John CD gets the remaining five.

Your soon-to-be ex loves anything Ikea—even their meatballs!—and therefore gives the shelf thirty-five points. He gives both the drill and the ramen noodles ten points. Last, the Elton John CD gets forty-five points, because your ex believes that "Daniel" is his (or her) theme song.

	YOU	EX
Elton John CD	5	45
Drill	10	10
Bookshelf	30	35
Ramen noodles	55	10

Step 3: Divide the possessions so that the person who gave each thing the most points gets it. So, this means you get the noodles and your soon-to-be ex gets the bookshelf and the CD. Hold off on dividing items where the points were tied (in this case, that would be the drill).

Step 4: Add up how many points what you got is worth to you. Your noodles were fifty-five points, so you are left with fifty-five points. Your soon-to-be ex, however, ended up with eighty points. (Jerk!) Because you are the one with fewer points, you get to take the tied item, the drill, in order to try to even the scale. But you still have only sixty-five to your rival's eighty.

Step 5: To make everything a bit more even, you need to liquidate one (or more) of the objects to which you both gave the most similar point value, and then split the cash. The actual algorithm has some kind of complicated formula for this part, but who has the time? In this case, let's say the item you choose to turn into cash is the Ikea bookshelf. So, if you get fifty bucks for the shelves on eBay, you'll walk away from the relationship with twenty-five dollars, a drill, and enough ramen to last a cold, cruel winter.

I'm not a witch, I'm your wife.
And after what you just said,
I'm not even sure I want to be that anymore.
—VALERIE,
THE PRINCESS BRIDE

Breakup Survey Results

We polled more than five hundred people across the country to determine their attitudes about breaking up.

What was the cause of your last breakup?

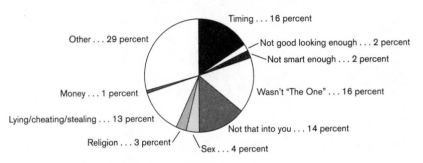

Among the "Other" reasons were:

"She was obsessed with her cat."

"We hated each other."

"Drugs."

"He was married."

"He decided he was a woman."

"She is crazy, and thought all problems were my fault."

"Possessive/controlling."

"Long distance."

"Emotional unavailability."

"Angelina Jolie."

"Midlife crisis."

"Commitment-phobe."

"My girlfriend joined a secret society to which I was not admitted."

"The ex returned."

When you are being dumped, would you prefer that your future ex tell you the truth about the cause or lie to spare your feelings?

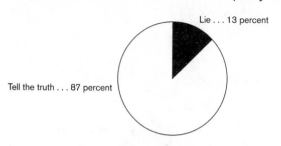

Lie . . . 13 percent

Tell the truth . . . 87 percent

After a breakup, I have:

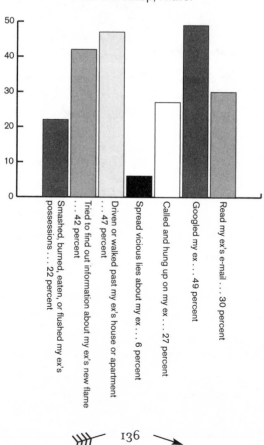

Smashed, burned, eaten, or flushed my ex's possessions . . . 22 percent

Tried to find out information about my ex's new flame . . . 42 percent

Driven or walked past my ex's house or apartment . . . 47 percent

Spread vicious lies about my ex . . . 6 percent

Called and hung up on my ex . . . 27 percent

Googled my ex . . . 49 percent

Read my ex's e-mail . . . 30 percent

I've told a lie to get out of a relationship:

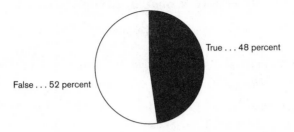

I've tried to get someone to dump me
so that I wouldn't have to do the dumping:

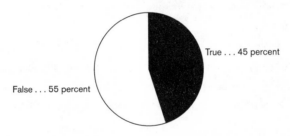

Irregardless, ex-boyfriends are just off-limits to friends.

I mean that's just like the rules of feminism.

—GRETCHEN WIENER, *MEAN GIRLS*

>>>— My Worst Breakup →

by Gregory Galloway

It was the Rasputin relationship—no matter how hard we tried to kill it, it wouldn't die. We tried poisoning it, drowning it, hacking it to pieces, but nothing sent us toward our happier, separate lives. Something stronger than our mutual desire to part kept us bound together. It was the rent.

We'd been living together in a studio apartment in the Village for almost a year, and after a few months of marathon arguments we decided to call it quits in early December.

Maybe it was the Christmas season, filled as it always is with misplaced hope, false optimism, and unrealistic expectations, or perhaps it was the daunting prospect of living alone, but after looking at apartments separately, we signed a lease on a two-bedroom apartment together. "I can't imagine not being with you," she said. It turned out that she had greatly underestimated the powers of her imagination. I came home one night in mid-January and found her painting the apartment with her new boyfriend.

I retreated to the extra bedroom and started looking again for my own place. The only problem was that my (very) meager salary only gave me a narrow window of opportunity to move out, before the next month's rent was due. She ended up breaking up with the painter friend and February came and went. By March I was dating someone else and became more determined to move out. In order to free some extra cash, my ex-girlfriend/current roommate and I decided to rent out the spare bedroom.

I somehow landed on the couch—which was a good four inches shorter than I am—where I stayed until August, when a call came from a good friend of mine who had a large two-bedroom place on the Upper West Side. His fiancée had ended things by dramatically throwing the engagement ring out the fourteenth-floor window. In one long, bewildering day we moved her out and me in; the long relationship nightmare was over. Two days later, the girlfriend who had patiently tolerated an awkward, ugly situation since March dumped me. At least I didn't have a lease; it was all month-to-month.

Gregory Galloway is the author of *As Simple as Snow*, a novel about love and loss. His last breakup was in 1995.

Love never dies a natural death.
It dies because we don't know how to replenish its source.
It dies of blindness and errors and betrayals.
It dies of illness and wounds;
it dies of weariness, of withering, of tarnishing.

—ANAÏS NIN

From the Trenches:
Best Breakup Lines

That's the spirit. Thank you.
Thank you for your honesty.
Now fuck off and die, you fucked-up slag.
—LARRY IN *CLOSER*

We surveyed veteran dumpers and dumpees around the country to ask them to share the best and worst breakup lines they've ever given or received.

"I said, 'You're sucking my will to live.'" Melissa, 30

"He told me, 'My mom won't let me see you anymore.'" Donna, 29

"After I told her that I had a problem with being monogamous, I added that I had a problem dating a woman who sleeps around. That pretty much ended things." Andrew, 41

"The best line used on me was when she said, 'I still love you'. . . the worst was the part that followed: 'but [this new guy] is just soooo cute!'" Lloyd, 46

"He was on drugs and I told him we shouldn't see each other anymore. I said, 'I don't want you to have a bad trip, but this has to end.'" Samantha, 24

"He said, 'It's like I love you, but I don't.'" Sarah, 29

"I told him, 'I just want to be alone for a while, I need to be happy by my-self." Abby, 23

"I checked my e-mail from my boyfriend when I was in Croatia (I was backpacking through Europe) and he said, 'I think we need to talk because I'm not sure we're on the same page or even reading the same book.' So I called him from Croatia, which meant I spent eighty-five dollars for him to tell me it was over." *Kristi, 23*

"She said, 'You are treating me badly. I do not accept being treated badly. I am leaving. Good-bye.'" *Charles, 38*

"He said, 'You're too short for me and I don't like the shape of your genitals.'" *Elizabeth, 29*

"I suggested she find somebody else to shit on." *George, 30*

"He told me he didn't think we should have sex anymore." *Morrigan, 33*

"I told her, 'There is a reason I've been single this long.'" *Mel, 34*

"In my last breakup my ex told me, 'I think we should just call this even.'" *Massiel, 25*

"He told me to grow some breasts." *Annie, 26*

"I knew it was over when she proclaimed, 'I am having his baby.'" *Jake, 36*

"I said, 'You smell like broccoli.'" *Caroline, 30*

"He said, 'I'm a rock. You need a tree.'" *Jen, 34*

"'I haven't been treating you very well,' he said, 'so maybe we shouldn't continue.'" *Ann, 35*

"She said, 'Making you happy isn't making me happy.'" David, 35

"I said, 'You're jeopardizing my sobriety.'" Lindsay, 25

"I said, 'I have a crush on my friend Amanda.'" Anna, 31

"He said he needed time to think. What he meant was that he needed time to move out of his house into his fiancée's house before the wedding." Amy, 28

"He said, 'If we stay together, we're just going to get married, and I'm not ready for that.'" Rose, 31

"I just said, 'See you soon, take care.'" Robb, 33

"She told me, 'No one could have as much sex as you want. I just don't have that much time in the day.'" Paul, 39

"He said, 'I'm breaking up with you because my sister told me to.'" Jen, 28

"He said, 'I think I just need to be single . . . you were my first serious relationship. Now I need to be single, you know, "sow my wild oats," so to speak.'" Carla, 30

"I said, 'I still want you in my band, but I just don't think we should have sex anymore.'" Erika, 28

"He said, 'Before you can be comfortable with anyone else you're going to learn to be comfortable with yourself.'" Claire, 25

"She said, 'I pretty much don't like you anymore.'" Fred, 31

WHAT NOT TO DO AFTER A BREAKUP

Don't . . . burn down your ex's house.

But no one would ever do that! Or would they?

On March 19, 2005, a home went up in flames on Main Street in Newport, Kentucky, following the resident's breakup with twenty-five-year-old James Poe. According to the local news stations, there was some question as to who began the fire until the ex-girlfriend came home and told police that Poe had just text-messaged her, saying, "I'm burning down your house."

How about instead of doing this, you try:

Making a campfire. Throw any letters your ex sent you into the flames. Then roast a marshmallow.

"She told me, 'I'm getting back together with my ex. You remind me of my brother.'" Nick, 34

"She said, 'Maybe someday I'll get my head together.'" Michael, 30

"This one guy gave me U2's 'Another Time, Another Place.' From this I was supposed to take a hint." Lynn, 36

"He said, 'It bothers me you have green eyes.'" Ekaterina, 19

"He said, 'You deserve someone who wants to spend time with you.'" Jordan, 22

"My ex said, 'I don't feel worthy of you.'" Sarah, 24

"'You are a great girl,' he said. 'I am going to regret this.'" Anne, 27

"You're a really nice guy, but what you really need is a therapist, not a girl-friend." Caitlin, 24

"I told him, 'Look, I have to be honest, it's the sex. I faked it (every time) because it was so boring, I just wanted to get it over with.'" Dana, 17

"He said, 'You don't love me like I love you.'" Chloe, 26

"I said, 'It IS you, not me. From A to Z and back to A again, it's you.'" Jackie, 28

Everything Else You Ever Wanted to Know about Breakups (but Were Afraid to Ask Dr. Phil)

It isn't enough for your heart to break
because everybody's heart is broken now.
—ALLEN GINSBERG

Breakup etiquette—how to do it, when to do it, where to do it, what to wear when you're doing it—has perplexed great thinkers from Socrates to Dr. Laura. In the preceding pages, we have tried to clarify as much as possible. Yet we didn't have room to answer some of your most difficult questions, until now . . .

When breaking up with someone I care about but don't want to marry, should I tell the truth or lie to spare the person's feelings?

ANNA JANE: Truth. If you lie, chances are that once your potential ex gets over the initial hurt—and there will be hurt even if you lie—he is going to sense that there was a piece of the puzzle missing. You're better off coming clean early than having to retrace your steps later.

FLINT: Lie like you're a politician on election day. People say they want the truth during a breakup (87 percent, according to our breakup survey), but this is the real lie. What good is that truth to you? If someone tells you that you didn't make her happy, or that you're too cynical, or that you make love like a sloth, what are you supposed to do with that? The fact is, if you try to change to please future lovers, you will only end up making yourself miserable, and they will recognize you for the phony you've become. So, during a breakup, lie and spare the other person's feelings. They'll be better off in the long run.

Should you break up at your place or your soon-to-be ex's?

FLINT: Your soon-to-be ex's, so you can flee when you're ready.

ANNA JANE: I agree—if you're the dumper, you're better off being at your soon-to-be ex's place, so that you're not in the position of having to throw him or her out when you're done doing the dumping. However, if possible, a private, neutral place is best so that no one feels his personal territory has been soiled. Karaoke booths can often be rented by the hour . . .

What sort of clothes should I wear to the breakup?

FLINT: Loose-fitting, possibly something cotton. And you don't want to look sexy. Ease the pain by making sure that last image in your soon-to-be ex's mind is of you looking terrible.

ANNA JANE: We're not on the same page with this one. Why would you want to look terrible? You don't need to be in black tie, but I think if you're the one ending a relationship, you want to go into it feeling as confident as you can, and dressing in a way that'll make you feel good about yourself is an easy way to build confidence. If you're the one getting dumped, you want to look your best too—you want your soon-to-be ex to walk away with an image of you looking amazing burned onto his or her brain. As a dumpee, one of the few things you have power over in the breakup is the degree to which your soon-to-be ex is going to be filled with regret and remorse.

Is it ever appropriate to break up in a public place, like a restaurant?

FLINT: No. And you should never dump someone after they bought you dinner. If you want to end it, be prepared to at least foot the bill for a meal.

ANNA JANE: Not if you can help it. And while we're on the topic of money, if the dumpee is going to have to go home alone after a split, it's nice of the dumper to pay for the cab or airfare.

Should you have a precomposed breakup speech or wing it?

FLINT: You should have talking points. Don't write it out word for word, but know your main points and stick to them. Write them on your arm if you must, or get a friend to stand behind your soon-to-be-ex holding cue cards.

ANNA JANE: If you really feel the need to compose the whole thing and then memorize it, you're probably better off just writing a letter and sending it or handing it to your soon-to-be ex.

If, during the breakup, your lover has a complete breakdown, do you stay and comfort her or him, or do you flee like a criminal leaving the scene?

ANNA JANE: Stay and do a little comforting—chances are you haven't suddenly stopped caring for him or her entirely. Treat the person like you'd treat a friend. If you think he or she is really such a mess that being alone for the night would be unwise, encourage the dumpee to get a friend to come over.

FLINT: No! Run! Run for your life! It may seem cruel, but it's even more cruel to pretend to comfort the person you just screwed over. They need to get used to you not being there for them.

Should you get your stuff during the breakup or come back at a later date?

FLINT: Take all your stuff right then. You do not want to have to go back to the scene of the crime.

ANNA JANE: If we're talking about items that are easily moveable, belongings should be sorted; anything that's going to require a U-haul can be gotten later. If your soon-to-be ex is breaking up with you on your turf, it can be especially cathartic to make sure they take their toothbrush with them when they leave.

FLINT: What? If a girl ever left a toothbrush at my place, I would immediately break up with her. And I'm speaking as the son of a dentist.

What's the best part of breaking up?

ANNA JANE: The best part is the way that the breakup can act as a truth serum, and you can find yourself getting all sorts of things off your chest with none of the consequences that existed while you were still invested in making things work. Now, you can finally tell your lover all those things you've been saying behind his back.

FLINT: The best part of breaking up is Folgers in your cup. Wait, that's waking up. The breakup itself is hell, pure unadulterated hell, but if you spend the breakup picturing all the new women you will see naked in the days and weeks to come, you might just find yourself smiling, until you actually get out there and realize you're not seeing anyone naked outside of Scores for a long time.

〉〉〉—   **A Breakup Letter**   ⟶

by Lynn Harris

Dear Daniel,

I heard you and Lisa[1] moved to Dallas.[2]

So now I won't run into you—oh wait, I never would have run into you, because you never leave work.

Speaking of which, I also heard you made partner. That's because I actually heard you, all the way from Dallas rubbing your palms together and hissing, "Soon my power will be complete."

Hey, do you remember saying that when you told me you loved me, you "meant it at the time"?

Well, when I told you I forgave you, I meant it at the time.

Years later, it still kills me—when I think about it, which is whenever I'm reminded that shitty mean people get stuff they don't deserve—that there are things I never said to your face. Back then, for the sake of my dignity and get-this-over-with closure, I let you off too easily. My only real "statement" was, when I collected my stuff while you were at the office, to leave your goddamned clichéd Monets and Wyeths all a teeeeeny bit crooked. Elegant of me; too good for you.

It's not THAT things ended, Daniel, it's HOW things ended. Eight months together. Paris with your parents, talk of sapphires vs. emeralds, combined-income math. Then yes, things started to get where's-this-really-going weird.

(continues)

〉〉〉—   149   ⟶

But that does not make it okay to disappear—verily, to LEAVE THE STATE for that exceedingly important case WITHOUT TELLING ME. I know, you said you "honestly didn't have a moment" to call. Even IF that were true, which it could have been if it were 30 years ago when there were no cell phones and only NASA had email, you honestly do have a fucking secretary.

Later that week, when you still didn't call even though you KNEW I had gone home to my parents' to PUT MY DOG TO SLEEP? Here's the thing. As long as she is still officially your girlfriend, if she goes home to put her beloved fifteen-year-old family dog to sleep, you must call her. It is the law.

I broke up with you that dog weekend. By myself. I just didn't get around to telling you until you, you know, had a moment.

Also, between the last time I didn't send this letter and now, I found out you also have two kids. That's lovely; what are their names? You can get back to me if you don't remember.

Love,

Lynn

[1]Name has been changed because I hate the fact that her name is actually really cool.
[2]Name has been changed to protect Miami.

Lynn Harris is cocreator, with Chris Kalb, of the award-winning Web site BreakupGirl.net.

———

PART THREE

Get Over It

Give me a dozen such heartbreaks,
if that would help me lose a couple of pounds.

—COLETTE

Congratulations, you've made it through the breakup. The proverbial fat lady—who may or may not be your mother-in-law—has sung. So now it's over, right?

Of course not!

Once you've seen someone naked once, you should be able to see that person naked again as many times as you want. After all, you can see him or her naked in your imagination. Or, if your ex is Paris Hilton, you can see her naked everywhere!

It's not commonly discussed, because it's depressing, but the truth of the matter is that the relationships that really touched you are ones you might never get over. Never ever. It's very possible that one day you will be ninety and living in Boca Raton and you'll stare into the eyes of your spouse over shuffleboard and think, "I should never have broken up with Chris in '97."

So, unlike most books about relationships, we're not going to attempt to tell you how to get over it. Why? Because it might never happen. The pain may subside and the hurt will become less raw, but it will still be there.

That's right—we're going to share with you an undeniable, rarely discussed truth: *you don't have to get over it.*

Sure, we called this section "Get Over It," but notice we left off any words that might actually apply a "how to" aspect to this section. Why? Because, like everyone else who was ever born, we have no freaking idea how to get over it. We've written a book on the topic, and we still cry about our own romantic failures. We drunk dial, we Web stalk, and sometimes we drive by our ex's house to see if there is a foreign car in the driveway. (Actually, only Flint does that;

Anna Jane prefers calling and hanging up when her ex answers, after blocking the Caller ID, of course.)

In short, when it comes to love lost, we are like you: irrational and insane.

On the other hand, irrationality and insanity aren't all bad. Consider Vincent Van Gogh. Sure, he lost an ear because of a bad relationship, but without that irrationality and insanity could he have produced all those masterpieces? These are the very manias that lead to greatness, romantic and otherwise.

The lunacy so many of us experience after a breakup is just part of the whole relationship cycle. It's kind of like the romantic afterbirth: messy and gross but a necessary reality. Purging isn't always pretty. And if the breakup doesn't hurt at all, it probably means the relationship didn't mean all that much to you in the first place.

So if there is no Jenny Craig for getting over a breakup (yet), how do you deal?

One thing is to remember that your hurt is a lot more about you and your own ego than it is about the other person. We love someone in part because they reflect back to us things we like about ourselves. It can cause a pretty good bruise if the person who loved you announces there's no longer anything likable about you.

Another thing is to realize that not every relationship can be a success. Otherwise, you might be married to your kindergarten boyfriend—you know, the one who everyone called "The Wedgie King."

If not every relationship can succeed, this means that some are going to be utter failures that will leave you drenched in regret and primed for suffering. But the postrelationship misery can act as a reminder to choose wisely next time. When you're down in the dumps after a failed affair, you'll remember that in the future it might be a bad idea to pursue just anyone if you are going to have to get on meds to get over him or her. In fact, if getting over a breakup weren't so painful, we might run around breaking up with every single person we ever meet, never putting in the effort to work out problems in a relationship—effort that can lead to a stronger bond and more love.

But most important, you need to try to accept that your ex served a purpose in your life even if he or she wasn't the one you're going to spend the rest of your life cuddled up with on the couch.

Think of your ex like Atari. It was a great game system and, if it weren't for Atari, you never would have met Nintendo. So Atari got old. So you got tired of having Kong throw barrels at your feet all day. That doesn't mean it wasn't great while it lasted. That doesn't mean that Atari didn't serve its purpose and can't get you twenty bucks on eBay.

Of course, if all this reasoning doesn't help relieve your pain, you can just decide your ex is an evil uber-villain who's single-handedly responsible for all of the world's hunger, poverty, and war. You played no role whatsoever in the end of your relationship. They say no one is perfect, but you are. In fact, you're so damn perfect that you're going to wrangle bravely with the postbreakup pain with us in order to try to lasso the hurt.

Like we said, we can't tell you how to get over it, but in the following pages, we'll make some suggestions informed

PROFILES IN NOT-A-LOT-OF-COURAGE

Liza Minnelli

Singer Liza Minnelli, daughter of the great Judy Garland, has loved and left—or been left by—four husbands in the past forty years; by Hollywood standards, this is a rather conservative number of mates. However, her track record is notable because of one thing: pretty much all her lovers were either gay, or gayish, which is especially interesting considering her father was rumored to prefer men and her mother is idolized by many homosexuals. Her first divorce was from famously gay singer/songwriter Peter "Don't Cry Out Loud" Allen. Legend has it that he spent their wedding night with another guy. Next up was Jack Haley Jr., who wasn't a "friend of Dorothy" as far as we know, but he was the son of the guy who played the Tin Man in the gay cult classic *The Wizard of Oz,* a movie in which her mom starred.

Then she divorced a supposedly straight sculptor named Marc Gero, because he wasn't supporting her efforts to sober up. Last came the inimitable David Gest, who purports straightness but also boasts a collection of Shirley Temple memorabilia and chose Michael Jackson as his best man at their wedding. After their divorce, Gest claimed she'd beaten him up.

Rounding out the gayness connections of this breakup maven is her onetime relationship with Kiss's Gene Simmons, who is heterosexual, despite his fondness for makeup. Interestingly, he's been with another gay icon or two (Cher and Diana Ross, among others). She also once broke up with Mikhail Baryshnikov, who *isn't* gay . . . but *is* a ballerina.

by our own history of attempting foolishly to do just that. We'll help you remember that it does no good to second-guess yourself. The relationship is over; it's history. The best you can do is keep reminding yourself that it wasn't you, it was your stinking ex.

Facts and Fictions about Your Terrible, Horrible, No Good, Very Bad Breakup

You just gotta get back on the horse, Coop.

You gotta giddy up, horsy!

—SUMMER, *THE O.C.*

When you're going through a breakup, suddenly everyone around you is spewing truisms and ego boosters. They all think they know best because, amazingly, they all once went through a similar breakup. What are the chances!

Of course, if they'd stop and think about it, they'd remember that they didn't enjoy being plastered with clichés or supposedly soothing advice during their own moments of sorrow . . . and they also wouldn't appreciate hearing you rip their exes apart, since chances are they weren't positive they weren't still going to end up with the loser.

Here is our attempt to untangle the knots of facts and fictions you'll most likely hear after your breakup:

Subject	Fictions	Facts
DATING	"You just need to get back on the horse."	You're going to have to get on a lot of horses before you can stay on one, especially if you insist on talking to the horse about how great things were with your ex.
SEX	"You're not going to get over someone until you're under someone new."	This one is actually true to an extent. However, getting under someone new just for a roll in the hay might only help you get over your ex till the rooster crows in the morning. It's going to take getting under someone you find you really care about in order to truly get over your ex.
FISH	"There are a lot of fish in the sea."	The ocean is swimming with disease.
GRIEVING	"It'll take one month for every year you're together."	You might never completely get over it, but it'll get easier when you fall for someone new. However, it might get harder if your ex falls for someone new first and you bump into them in the mall while you're shopping for socks alone.
FRIENDS	"Your friends will be there to guide you through this difficult period. That's what friends are for."	Your friends will be there to guide you through this difficult period, for a while, but even good friends will put up with only so much sniveling and will begin giving advice that they would never take themselves. Friends who are single might stick around a little longer.
MEETING SOMEONE ELSE	"You can do better."	You'll probably do worse before you do better.

Subject	Fictions	Facts
STALKING	"It's important to make a clean break."	It's important to drive by your ex's house repeatedly until you're certain that he or she is sleeping with someone new.
THE LOVE OF YOUR LIFE	"When you meet the right person, you'll just know."	You didn't know last time. Why will the next time be any different?
MASTURBATING	"Masturbation is a healthy way to remain sexually satisfied during the long, hard months after a breakup."	Perhaps, but when those pictures of the ex with someone new pop into your head, it really kills it, or it makes it hotter.
REVENGE	"The best revenge is living well."	The best revenge is replacing your ex's shampoo with Nair.
THE FUTURE	"You're better off without him."	Then why do you miss him so much?

The Grossman-Wainess Guide

to Rock Bottom . . .

It's Cheaper than *Frommer's!*

Are you planning a vacation but have no one to vacation with because you're in the middle of a devastating breakup? Forget Venice; don't even think about Jamaica. The only vacation destination for you is Rock Bottom.

We know: it has a bad reputation. Ever since the tragic "drive-by" incident of 2002 in which you mistook the gardener's car for your ex's new lover's, you've wanted to book a ticket elsewhere. There's the high suicide rate, and the riots during prohibition.

But, the fact is, everyone goes to Rock Bottom sometime. So stop putting off those vacation plans, stop pretending you're okay, and come join us for a week, month, or (yikes) year at sunny Rock Bottom. The time to book that ticket is now!

Leave your cameras at home. You won't want pictures of this. And, above all, never forget: Rock Bottom is a fine place to visit but no place to live.

Where to Stay

You're desperate, you're crying, you're cheap, and so it's tempting just to curl up in a little ball on a busy street. Don't be fooled. Rock Bottom has many lovely places for you to stay. Other than Heartbreak Hotel, there are no hotels at Rock Bottom—that stuff is for lovers—but that doesn't mean you have stay in your apartment (if you had a home, you probably wouldn't be at Rock Bottom). Go to a friend's, or just follow a random person who lives in a fancy house. They'll let you in. They'll feed you. Tell them the story of how you came to Rock Bottom.

What to Eat

The cuisine at Rock Bottom simply cannot be beat. Famous for its many varieties of bourbon, nicotine, beef jerky, turkey jerky, cake, and

PARIS: *"Maybe I shouldn't go. I mean, what if I fall for him and he doesn't like me?"*

RORY: *"Then you'll find someone else."*

PARIS: *"But what if there is no one else?"*

RORY: *"Then you'll buy some cats."*

—*THE GILMORE GIRLS*

ice cream, you would be remiss if you did not indulge yourself while at Rock Bottom. The creamier the better, the higher calorie count the better. Since you won't be driving while at Rock Bottom, drink until your heart is content, and ingest nicotine as if you were actually a smoker, or a cowboy.

Of course, there are some healthy establishments at Rock Bottom. In theory, this makes sense. The better you eat, the better you feel, and the quicker you can get out of Rock Bottom and be attractive to new people. But do you really care about that right now? No! You're at Rock Bottom! You can't think past five minutes from now, and so you should eat, drink, and smoke like you only have five minutes left on this planet.

Oh, and there's an Arby's. Try the roast beef. We don't know how the Zoning Commission missed that one.

What to Do

Everybody has their favorite Rock Bottom activities, but we think all good things at Rock Bottom begin with the drive-by, or the walk-by. You know, slowly walking or driving past your ex's house, apartment, or cubicle. This isn't stalking; you're just trying to see what they're up to, and who they're up to it with. If you see something you did not want to see during the drive-by (say, a tall French stranger kissing your ex on the neck and/or buttocks), you might want to retire to your chambers with the collected works of the Smiths, some soft-core pornography, rocky road ice cream, and the leftover bourbon from dinner. After doing this for a while, you might be tempted to check on the nightlife at Rock Bottom. But beware: you're not ready. The nightlife is dark and seedy and dangerous. This is no time to be hitting up the clubs.

We've heard of all kinds of crazy things being done at Rock Bottom—quitting jobs, buying puppies, hacking into your ex's e-mail, streaking, trying to eat yourself to death, trying to eat your ex, becoming a hermit, listening endlessly to Herman's Hermits, joining the circus, trying to set the *Guinness Book* record for number of tears shed, trying to set the *Guinness* record for number of Guinesses consumed, climbing a mountain, sleeping with people you meet at Starbuck's, and on and on—and there's nothing wrong with it. This is adult spring break. It's your chance to act like a complete and utter fool. The important thing is, what happens at Rock Bottom stays at Rock Bottom— because wallowing can only last so long.

Stages of (Good) Grief, Charlie Brown

Dear Baby, Welcome to Dumpsville.
Population: You.
—HOMER SIMPSON

Life is chock-full of stages. There are stages of mourning. There are stages of growing a beard. So why shouldn't there be stages of getting over a broken heart?

You might feel like you're the first one to have ever gone down this spiral staircase of loneliness and hurt. But you're not. There's a crowd of people waiting for you at the bottom, and they've all had to go through the same stages of grief that you're going to go through.

What exactly are you in for? Something like this:

Stage 1: Denial

You stand in front of your former love, slack-jawed. "You're breaking up with me? You? Are breaking up? With me?" The moments and days after being dumped tend to be filled with disbelief. You can't help but wonder: *How did I not see the signs? Shouldn't I be the one breaking it off with this loser? Will I ever love again?*

But then you begin to answer these questions, bringing us to . . .

Stage 2: Anger

At this point, you realize you didn't see the aforementioned signs because your ex is a lying, cheating snake who was hiding them from you. You should've been the one to break it off! You're the cuter one! You're the smarter one! You're better at Scrabble! Yet you're the one who is being left. So what do you do? You plot murder and sabotage. You contemplate elaborate forms of revenge but then settle for hurling rumpled tissues at the floor. (This is also your cat's favorite breakup stage.) Your new personal mantra is:

How can I love when I'm so filled with rage? The asshole has taken away my ability to feel anything.

But, of course, anger eventually becomes tiresome, and dissolves into . . .

Stage 3: Bargaining

Like puberty, this is a humiliating and painful stage. You'll know you've entered it when you begin begging your ex to take you back. After all, the only one who can ease the pain is the one who caused it, right? "I can change," you say. "I'll do anything. I'll start brushing my teeth on weekends!" You believe you really *can* change—you were *born* to conform to someone else's ideals—but your ex isn't receptive. So this will eventually beget . . .

Stage 4: Drunk Dialing

The bargaining has failed, negotiations have stalled, and your relationship has fizzled to the point where you can now call only when you're with your buddy Stolichnaya. But you have good friends, and friends don't let friends drink and dial, mainly because after a while they'll stop finding it funny. You deny it the next day by saying your phone was in your pants and the call was totally accidental, but your former flame isn't buying it. So you find a quieter way to reach out and touch your ex when you sober up (mmmm . . . touch your ex). This would be . . .

Sage 5: Obsessing

You should be working or sleeping, but instead you are spending hours looking up your ex's name on the Internet. You drive by your ex's house, just to see if the lights are on or if there's a strange car in the driveway. You call your ex and then hang up. This eventually morphs into you telling your friends every detail of the breakup. You talk so much about your ex that his or her name starts to lose meaning. It's kind of like saying "Lindsay Lohan" twelve times straight. After you do this for a few weeks, you hit . . .

Stage 6: Depression

What's the point of even getting out of bed? What was the point of *Herbie: Fully Loaded?* You're warm under your covers and you have cookies. And cable! Why do anything ever again when you can stay in bed and watch *Gilligan's Island?* It's like staying home from school when you're a kid, only then you weren't aware of the hopelessness of love and dating and mating and e-mail. Suddenly, you realize that this is the first moment of clarity you've ever had in your whole life, and now you finally understand that life is just a pointless scam and we're all as insignificant as ants, and if one little ant dies of a broken heart after not having changed his clothes for two weeks straight, does anyone really care? If only someone would just step on us and end all this misery and suffering. Then comes the real epiphany: the cookies are stale. *Can't eat, can't breathe, can't even enjoy* Gilligan's Island. You would go back to sleep but the sheets are full of crumbs. Geez, just put the goddamn radio together already, Professor. You're depressed, so very depressed . . . and then one day you arrive at . . .

Stage 7: Object Fetishism

Just when you thought you couldn't get any lower, you start crying because you find that stuck to your refrigerator door is a Willie Nelson magnet your ex gave you. You two discovered Willie *together!* Listening to Willie will never be the same. Going to the refrigerator will never be the same. Good thing you've started keeping food under the bed . . . right next to that vintage stuffed Smurf doll! Oh, no! You and your ex loved the Smurfs! Remember that time you bought it together at that county fair? Remember how you both kind of thought Smurfette was hot? The Smurfs will never be the same! And now your doll will have to be raised in a single-parent household. But then, as you're trying to come to terms with this travesty, you suddenly find yourself at . . .

I've never been married, but I tell people I'm divorced so they won't think something's wrong with me.

—ELAYNE BOOSLER

Stage 8: John Cusack

Say Anything is on. Gilligan and the Skipper may have only made you feel worse—even on a desert island, Ginger and Mary Ann can't get any action—but John Cusack makes you feel so much better. If John Cusack can get his heart broken, anyone can. And if he can convince Diane Court to love him, anything is possible. What's that salty substance coming from your eyes? Love *is* possible! But you're not ready to post that online personal just yet. So first you turn to . . .

Stage 9: Reminiscing

You start remembering the good things, like that one time you guys had really great sex. Then you start thinking about the not-so-good things, like that there was only one time you guys had really great sex. Then you realize you could be having decent sex by yourself, which brings us to . . .

Stage 10: Excessive Masturbation

For more on this step, please consult your local physician. Then you'll be ready for . . .

Stage 11: Rebounding

After all that self-love, you're ready for the love of a stranger. So comb your hair, whiten your teeth, and get out there, hot stuff! It doesn't really matter whom you pick, as long as he or she is unlike your ex in every possible way. Put those beer goggles on, it's time to party! The next morning, you wake up hung over in a stranger's bed, and your underwear is missing. As you search for your Calvins, you can't help but feel like you might be approaching . . .

THE BREAKUP REGISTRY

So you've broken up, and you're having serious withdrawal . . . from your electric can opener.

Never fear: if marrying couples can register in order to fill their cupboards, divorcing couples can too. Why? Because we say so.

Most registries will drive you crazy with pictures of happy couples showing off their wares. Fortunately, there are a handful of Web sites where a future spouse isn't required in order to register for gifts.

http://www.theytookeverything.com
http://www.findgift.com/occasions/breakup-or-divorce
  Both these sites are specifically designed for people going through a breakup. They allow you to register for myriad breakup essentials—everything from a new television to a bag of potato chips to a warm and fuzzy security blanket. They also sell voodoo dolls.

http://www.mossonline.com
  This New York–based store has a registry available for single people whose exes took all the really cool stuff. The vintage Verner Panton chairs? Gone! If a Target replacement won't do, this is the site for you. When it asks you what kind of an event your registry is being created for, we suggest choosing "house warming."

http://www.felicite.com
  Felicite is mainly a Web site for couples getting married, but it does have an "other" category for those of us wanting to register solo. The site basically acts as a portal so that you can register for gifts from everywhere from Bloomingdale's to the Ferret Store—because, really, you might be heartbroken, but does your ferret need to suffer too?

http://www.walmart.com/wishlist
http://www.amazon.com/wishlist
  These sites are best suited for those who don't dig the idea of a formal registry but nevertheless would like to subtly suggest things they might like to get now that they've been left in the cold with not even a monogrammed towel to their name.

Stage 12: Anger (but Less So)

You're mad at your ex for making you drink all those beers and hook up with that loser from the bar that seemed really hot at the time but on further examination bears a disturbing resemblance to Pat from *Saturday Night Live*. Yet your anger has a distant quality to it. You can feel it breaking apart even as you are experiencing it. You're pissed off, but now you can eat and breathe and sleep without too much difficulty. At this point, you are ever so close to the final stage of grief . . .

Stage 13: Finding Someone New . . . and Better

It happens. It may take days, it may take months, it may even take fiscal quarters, but eventually you'll meet someone who makes every part of your body tingle. You'll grow. You'll change. And then one day you will run into the ex who sent you on that sad journey of grief once upon a time, and you will be amazed that this is that same someone who drove you to watch *Gilligan's Island*.

> *To fall in love is awfully simple,*
> *but to fall out of love is simply awful.*
> —BESS MYERSON

Web Stalking for Beginners

There's such a fine line between . . . stalking and, and being attentive,

and I was—I don't know—going for being attentive.

—HARRY SAWYER, *HAPPY, TEXAS*

It's an old story:

See Dick. See Dick kiss Jane. See Dick leave Jane.

Now, see Jane trail Dick's every move to make sure that he knows no happiness without her for as long as they both shall live.

With the advent of the Internet and cell phones, stalking an ex has never been more convenient.

Here's everything you need to know to be an expert ex-cum-PI:

Forethought, Forewarned

The best time to prep for a breakup is when things are going well (that is, before the desire to cheat sets in).

There are certain pieces of information that make stalking almost effortless. However, getting your hands on them while things are still all hugs and rainbow kisses might take strategizing.

If you really do stay together, then it won't seem weird later on to have these pertinent documents and numbers—sharing is what love is all about!

However, if you do break up, it'll be good to have your arsenal full just in case, since you never know what information on you your ex has stockpiled during your time together. Think of this as a purely defensive maneuver.

The following pieces of information can be used online or in local record offices to track an ex's movements and finances either after a relationship ends or during the relationship if/when you suspect cheating.

Driver's Licenses

The very first time in a relationship that a wallet is put on a table to pay for a meal or is plopped carelessly on a dresser it should be opened. Done postcoital, this can be done very coyly . . . unless cash is indeed about to be exchanged. The best way to go is to flip through your lover's cards and make comments about the mullet he has in his Texas A&M college ID card. Then pull out the driver's license and, if you can, pocket it so that you can sneak to the bathroom with a pen to copy down all the pertinent information on it—height, weight, middle name, driver's license number, and so on. All these can be useful if you decide to do some real *Magnum PI* tracking of the loser at some point in the future.

Cell Phone and Credit Card Bills

Open these when your ex is not around and write down the account numbers. Throw out the bill when done—your soon-to-be ex will simply think it's been misplaced. If found out, claim you thought it was yours. It's a good idea to do this with checks and pay stubs, too.

These will help you keep abreast of your ex's financial habits, so you'll be able to see if there's any major fluctuations to be noted. You could also use some of this information to steal money, but that could land you in jail, and we hear the ice cream flavors there are very limited.

Birthday, City of Birth, Mother's Maiden Name,
Personal Identification Number

Again, the best time to obtain all these is after sex. Preferably, it should be done while spooning. The best thing to do is to ask outright for this information. Just make sure not to ask for all the information at once. Subtlety is key. Try the following.

"Sweetie, what's your sign? Oh, so that would make your birthday when exactly? Wow! I know someone else born in March! Were you born in a hospital, too? No way! So was she! Wait, where was the hospital located? Oh. Hers was in Bucharest. Hey, what's your favorite TV show? And also, I was just wondering: what color do you like best? I see. Now, is that your mother's favorite color too? Oh, no reason—I just read once that sometimes people like the same color as their mother. She likes blue too? Amazing! Told you so. Hey, I bet I can't guess your mother's maiden name! Is it Smith? Lipschitz? Wow, this is hard. Noodlebaum! Okay, I give up. Oh! I wouldn't have guessed that. Huh. So, now let me see if I can guess your PIN . . ."

Now, take all this information and put it in a lockbox. The breakup lockbox. And not one of those combination lockboxes where the combination is "0-0-0-0."

Google

Google isn't just a search engine: it's a key postbreakup tool.

THINGS NO NEWLY SINGLE PERSON WANTS TO HEAR (BUT PROBABLY WILL)

"You're not getting any younger."

"You'll meet someone else when you least expect it."

"I could never understand what you were doing with her anyway."

"Maybe you should try lowering your standards."

"Yeah, I always had a feeling Leslie was cheating on you."

"John was a real catch—too bad he got away!"

"One day you'll look at all this and laugh."

"Now that you guys are through, could I get her number?"

"Many people never meet anyone, but live very full lives anyway."

"You only want to be with people who don't want to be with you."

The key to good Googling is diversifying your searches, and repeating them often, as the good people at Google are constantly expanding their searches to yield more hits. (Editor's note: We don't actually know anyone who works at Google, and they may not be good people, so if you're dating someone who works at Google, do not trust them.)

When we say diversify, we mean trying as many different combinations as possible.

Quotes are also important, as this will tell Google to look for a string of words and names and not for them individually.

So, after first trying a direct search for your ex ("Ima Major Ho"), you'll want to try doing the same search, but without the middle name. Then try using a middle initial. Then try reversing the first and last names. You should also plug in his or her e-mail address to see if anything comes up. Also try their street address, their phone number, and their preferred Web name—for example, "Bunny 345." With any luck, after doing all this, you'll find what you want to know—from how they did on a recent marathon to what porn DVD collection they're commenting on at Amazon. If nothing at all comes up regarding your ex, then you'll know they weren't worth stalking in the first place, as they are too much of a loser to ever have done anything meriting a mention anywhere.

If your ex has a common name like Joe Smith or shares a name with someone important like Carrot Top, it's a manageable problem. Say your ex's name happens to be George Bush and he happens not to be the forty-third president of the United States but is actually an assistant manager at the Gap. Try searching for "George Bush" and then use the minus sign before the word *president,* so your search will look like this:

"George Bush" "the Gap" - President

This should exclude most mentions of W.

Now, if you know the name of your ex's new flame, use it to go back and repeat all the steps above. Also make sure to search both names together. And remember, if someone doesn't show up on Google, they probably didn't exist in the first place.

Google also has a feature called "Images" (images. google.com) that will let you search for pictures of your ex and should be checked every time you conduct one of the above searches.

Web Sites

If you find a Web site that you think might belong to your ex or if you want to find out how it is the person writing the blog knows that your ex only wears yellow briefs, it's easy to figure out who owns the site. You need to conduct a "Who Is" search. BetterWhoIs.com is our favorite place to do this. Many of our exes keep blogs. Blogger.com is a good place to search to see if your ex happens to have one.

Take one friend of ours who recently discovered that her ex has a blog that he updates daily with news of his cats' feelings about dry versus wet food. This has helped her expedite the "moving on" process considerably.

Friendster, MySpace, Dating Sites, and Other Networking Services

It's a good idea to get onto MySpace or similar sites under a false name and request to be friends with your ex. They'll accept the request. Who doesn't want more friends!?

Because of the handy and easily updatable profile, this will show you where your ex is currently living, and if he or she is single.

On dating sites, you can try to find your ex by doing very narrow searches—search for people of their exact age, race, hair color, zip code, and so on. Now try e-mailing them there with a fake e-mail address, just for fun.

Once you find your ex's online dating screen name, you can try plugging it into the search engines at the sites True-Dater.com or LemonDate.com. Here, you can keep track of your ex's online dating activity by checking if anyone who has met your ex on the Internet has written a "review" of his or her profile.

Registries

Want to know if your ex is married, or is getting married, or was married three times before you met and never told you?

In this modern age of ours, all this and more can be found online.

Just log on to TheKnot.com or WeddingChannel.com, two wedding Web sites that catalog registries of newly married, soon married, and once married couples around the world.

That's right. You'll see that she's finally going to get that fondue set she always dreamed of. And remember how he used to joke about registering for Jackie Chan movies and power tools? Guess what, sister . . .

The only thing that can beat the joy of finding eternal love is being rewarded for it with a really good drill.

Just plug in the first and last names of your ex into the handy search boxes these sites provide and, with any luck, his or her name and the name of the intended will pop up. These sites automatically catalog the registries of major stores, so many couples don't even realize they are on it. But some do, and even go and use a special, easy feature they offer to make personalized wedding Web pages—there are pictures of the couple on them, along with cute details about how they met and their favorite sexual positions (okay, not really, but it's a good idea, right?).

If your ex's big day is about to arrive and you're feeling a little evil—and flush—why not order them a few of the gifts they've asked for (nonstick muffin pans! antifreeze ice scream scoops!) and then sign the online cards with anonymous names like "U. Suck" or "Yule B. De Vorced-Thistimenextyear."

And if you're feeling super evil, create a Web page through one of these sites for them. You can enter all the relevant information about the happy couple and upload any inappropriate photo you want. It's free, easy, and fun to forward around to your friends. Not that we'd know . . .

Instant Messenger

Keep your ex on your buddy list, and you'll be able to see when he or she is on- or offline. The ballsy can even sign up under a new IM name, and then can IM the ex while pretending to be someone else.

MedeaGirl: Hey! Is this Jason?
JJStud: LOL . . . Who are you?
MedeaGirl: It's [insert generic, generation-appropriate name]. We went to high school together.
JJStud: Yeah!
MedeaGirl: You were hot. ;) I loved how you [insert personal detail like "were able to use concealer to cover up herpes" or "could burp the alphabet"].
JJStud: That skill has not come in as handy as you'd think. Yeah, I think I remember you! You were hot, right? What have you been up to?

BREAKUP CUSTOMS

Judaism: Jew Get the Get?

According to traditional Hebrew law, only a man can initiate a divorce, and he can choose to do so for any reason or no reason. The divorce is complete the moment his wife receives the "get," which is a twelve-line handwritten bill stating that the marriage is terminated. Done under the supervision of a rabbi, the get is traditionally written on parchment with a quill pen and specifies the location of the couple by what body of water they live closest to. If a man can't get the woman to take the get from him, technically they are not divorced. However, some rabbis say that if he throws it and it lands within two feet of her, it is looked at as if she "accepted" it. Without a get, a woman cannot remarry.

So what if he goes off to war and never returns, but is also never found dead? In order to protect against this problem, sometimes a man will give his wife a provisional get before he goes off to war. What a mensch!

MedeaGirl: Not much. This and that. You? Want to send me some compromising naked photos of yourself?

Ladies and gentleman, a friendship has been born. TTYL.

The Single Guy:
Flint's Guide for the Newly Single Male

Every time you mention some guy that's a bastard [to a girl],
she'll tell you he has an inferiority complex.
Maybe he has,
but that still doesn't keep him from being a bastard.
—HOLDEN CAULFIELD, *CATCHER IN THE RYE*

Every boy wants a girl, until he gets her and discovers that he was significantly happier when he was single.

You can call it the "grass is always greener" syndrome, or you can admit the truth: there are innumerable joys to being an unfettered male, and these joys are greater than the delight a man gets from a relationship.

Are you ready for some football? Yes.

Are you ready for a girlfriend? No.

After a traumatic breakup, it's easy to be wistful. You begin pining for the days in which you and your shmoopie were holding hands at the zoo and making love before breakfast.

But, the reality is, for every time you and your one-time lady made love before breakfast, there was a time you had to waste an entire day at Bloomingdale's while she tried on hundreds of pairs of shoes that all looked exactly the same (and you had to pretend to be enthusiastic about every freaking new pair). For every time you held hands at the zoo, there was a time you had to watch a *Sex and the City* rerun even though the World Series was on (we get it, Samantha likes sex, Carrie likes clothes, and the brunette doesn't like anything!).

That was then, this is now. Now you're free! No more shoes, no more *Sex and the City.* This section is here to serve as a wake-up call to remind you of the joys of the single life.

After all, men were meant to roam free and spread their seed! When we're eighty and impotent and incontinent, it might be better to have a lover by our side.

But, until then, being single is pretty damn great.

So here's to the bachelor's paradise . . .

Have Sex with Multiple Partners

Presumably, one reason to have a relationship is to have regular sex. But this clashes with basic Darwinian principles of survival of the fittest (except in Kansas, where Darwin is no longer accepted). In order to have the best odds of propagating the species, one must sleep not with one woman but with many different women. Even sleeping with sisters makes evolutionary sense.

Yet somehow this behavior is frowned upon.

For women, many of whom have turned their backs on the basic scientific teachings of Darwin, good sex requires practice and an emotional connection. In other words, it can get better over the course of a relationship. But, for a man, achieving orgasm is a simple procedure. It doesn't get better with time. In fact, it gets worse. Trying new positions is nice, but not as nice as seeing a really hot girl naked for the first time.

In short, as long as you are not such a loser that you can never have sex when you're single (for instance, *Star Trek* fans, or me), your sex life will be better when you're unattached. The sex may be less frequent, but it will be a lot more exciting. The thrill of the chase is superior to any orgasm, now matter how Tantric. And the daydreaming about all the women you will soon bed isn't so bad either. So chase, brothers, chase! All too soon, you'll be with someone new—someone who doesn't want you sleeping with her sister—and you'll wish you had had more conquests when you were a free man.

Watch Sports Like It's Your Job

God created man, and then he created balls for men to play with. No, not those balls. Basketballs, baseballs, footballs, foosballs. Like all self-respecting men, there is nothing I enjoy so much as playing/watching/thinking about/ talking about sports. Which is why having a girlfriend is so troublesome. Because, no matter how cool she is, she is just not as cool as a game-saving tackle or a ninth-inning home run over the Green Monster.

So why not devote your newfound free time to your favorite home team?

When I have a girlfriend, a free Saturday might consist of such exciting events as shopping, going to the mall, shopping at the mall, talking, or seeing a movie starring Kate Hudson followed by shopping at the mall. Even if we do something potentially fun, like going to the beach, I will be unable to do the thing I really want to do when I'm at the beach: ogle young women in small bikinis.

In contrast, a free Saturday without a girlfriend typically consists of watching football or thinking about football or occasionally throwing a football at the beach. I can combine two favorite activities by "accidentally" throwing the football into a group of young women in small bikinis.

In my experience, women simply don't understand sports. And they certainly can't comprehend that from September through February my male brain processes information related only to a) the BCS rankings and b) the NFL playoff picture. I can smile and nod along with other conversations, but the whole time I'm thinking that this is an inferior discussion and this whole episode would be so much better if we were talking about the matchup problems presented by Michael Vick.

Of course, some women enjoy sports, both playing and watching them.

These are the worst women of all.

They fit into two categories. The first category is the sports-loving tomboy. The sports-loving tomboy is not sexy and is a poor substitute for a guy friend, because she has probably never played organized football and because you can't talk about chicks or eat a wheel of cheese while watching the game with her. The second category is the girlfriend who loves sports because you love them. She adopts your team because it brings her closer to you. Sadly, this too is not sexy. You resent her for distracting you from the game with her bosoms.

So, next time you're spending a perfectly sunny Saturday on the couch, with your hand down your pants, watching Reggie Bush streak down the sidelines, call your ex and tell her how happy you are that she is far, far away.

Spend Your Money on You

Let's be honest: when it comes to money, men get completely screwed, whether or not we are in a relationship. If we have a girlfriend, we are expected to buy them presents and pay for dinner and eventually purchase a condo for them and their cat, despite our job as assistant to the assistant manager at Blockbuster. If we're single, we are expected to pay for our dates, even if it's a blind date and she weighs three hundred pounds and has more body hair than we do. Yet a survey of at least five men has revealed that being single is still lighter on the wallet than being in a relationship, as long as you don't go out every night, take your dates only for drinks (dollar pitcher night!) rather than dinner, and date really anorexic girls.

The rest of your spare cash you can now spend on someone you really love: you.

Get a Lot of Sleep

According to scientists, the average male requires nine hours of sleep to maintain proper mental and physical health. When single, one can easily achieve this. Sure, there is the occasional booze-soaked crazy night that lasts until three in the morning, but you have the rest of the week to make up for the missed hours of rest. Your boss will understand; you got lucky! You need rest!

In a relationship, no such luck exists. The night consists of three parts, in no particular order: talking, cuddling, and sleeping. Depending on the relationship, talking and cuddling can take away two to four hours of time better spent sleeping. And that's not even including the dreaded middle-of-the-night cuddle, or the times that your partner's snoring wakes you up in the middle of the night.

That's why it is of extreme importance that the single male sleep as much as he can. He must gather his strength, storing it like a squirrel stores nuts, for that dark day in the future when he is again in a relationship, and is forced into mandatory snuggling all night long.

Eat Alone

Here is a fact that most men will not admit to their girl-friends: they would rather eat alone. For many men, the ideal meal can be purchased at 7-Eleven and consumed while watching *SportsCenter*. The more refined man orders from a gourmet restaurant—or cooks up his special spaghetti recipe that he claims is more than just spaghetti—and then quietly consumes it with a cold beer and a good book or sports clip. How eating got mixed up with talking remains a great mystery, but some historians have speculated that in homes where women were doing the cooking, they demanded a "how was your day" conversation as remuneration. Modern man continues to suffer through meal after meal in which he has absolutely nothing to say about his day and doesn't want to hear about anyone else's day but has to pretend he does in order to fill his body with nutrients.

The single male, by contrast, can eat in silence. Even better, he doesn't have to use a fork or a napkin. If he stains his shirt, he can just throw it away and buy a new one.

⟫⟩— **My Worst Breakup** ⟶

by Steve Almond

My central problem hasn't been in breaking up, but in refusing—owing to some toxic blend of conscious guilt and unconscious sadism—to break up. I am thinking, in particular, of an episode several years ago in which I refused to break up with my girlfriend, even though she lived halfway across the country and I didn't really love her anymore and even though I had begun a torrid affair with a woman who worked in my office.

No, rather than come clean, I allowed my girlfriend to fly to see me and then went on vacation with her, though every time she left the hotel room I called my new lover and spoke to her in a cooing, profane manner meant to suggest to her that, even though I was on vacation with my girlfriend, I really wanted to be with her, snuggling with her, doing the dirty things we did, and I was—couldn't she see this?—suffering, and I actually half expected that my new lover would feel some pity for me.

It was a despicable performance.

And when my girlfriend finally burst into the room and narrowed her eyes and said, *Who the hell are you talking to?* I covered the phone and said, *My mother, who else?*

Steve Almond is the author of *The Evil B.B. Chow, Candyfreak,* and *My Life in Heavy Metal.* For more details on his perversions, check out www.bbchow.com.

The Single Girl:
Anna Jane's Guide for the
Newly Single Lady

Men are rats, listen to me, they're fleas on rats,
worse than that, they're amoebas on fleas on rats.
I mean, they're too low for even the dogs to bite.
—FRENCHY TO SANDY, *GREASE*

If you're a woman and you've read Flint's guide, it should now be clear to you why being a single female can be so enjoyable. Some of the greatest women in history have opted to never settle down, and instead embraced the benefits of singledom—Emily Dickinson flew solo, as did Queen Elizabeth I and Catherine the Great, Amelia Earhart and Katharine Hepburn, Jane Austen, Florence Nightingale, Murphy Brown, Wonder Woman, and Lisa Simpson. Why? Because there are too many Flints in this world, my friends!

The Flints of the world whine about not getting enough action and then grouse about having to occasionally spend money on someone other than themselves. They want threesomes when most of them should consider themselves lucky to be half of a twosome. They make sweeping, ridiculous generalizations, like "women don't like sports" and "women only want to cuddle." They prefer eating fast food alone than having a conversation with someone who cares about them over a home-cooked meal.

It's possible your ex didn't fall into any of these male-chauvinistic traps. Maybe he was a specimen of boyfriend (or husband) perfection—but then why aren't you still together?

Chances are your newfound single life is going to be a vacation. Remember: scratch a happy, balanced woman in a relationship and you'll find one who can do just fine on her own. All too soon, you'll be coupled again—perhaps for good—and as happy as you may potentially be, you'll look back wistfully on your single days.

So enjoy them while you can.

Eat a Lot

Many men might not know this, but the fact is that most women like to eat—a lot. Sadly, too many ladies abstain from doing it around men. Scared of gaining weight, they order salads (when they'd like a burger), get vinaigrette on the side (when they'd honestly prefer ranch), and then they leave half of the food uneaten so as not to seem piggish. Some even forgo meals altogether in favor of nutrition shakes.

Ladies, now that you're single, this foolishness needs to stop.

Indulge. Eat what you want! If you want to eat a pint of Coffee Heathbar Crunch, go for it. If you want hot fudge on it, knock yourself out. Keep it all within reason and you're not going to get fat. You might gain a little, but you'll lose it—and hey, maybe you'll meet Mr. Right at Weight Watchers! Chances are, however, you won't get to that point: being single is going to afford you more time to hit the gym.

WHAT NOT TO DO AFTER A BREAKUP

Don't . . . try to kidnap your ex.

But no one would ever do that! Or would they?

In April 2005, thirty-six-year-old Sharon Ann Tonkin of New Zealand promised her car to a teenager if he'd help her kidnap her ex-boyfriend, John Timmins. She and the teen shot at him when he came home from work, then tied him up and wrestled him under a blanket in her car. But at some point during the joyride that followed, Timmins freed himself and ran into the woods.

How about instead of doing this, you try:

Holding your ex's aloe plant hostage. Then send ransom notes, with pictures of the plant in compromising situations.

And when you're in the supermarket loading up on Pringles, don't be surprised if Prince Charming asks for your number: a man who likes a girl who knows how to eat is a man that's worth eating with.

Stop Shaving

Girls, let your hair down! And no, I'm not talking about your ponytail. In the days and weeks after a breakup, we're allowed to enjoy a little hiatus from the Bic. Most of us women aren't shaving our pits and shins for a man; we're doing it because it makes us feel better about how we look and feel. I like being smooth, but I'm more likely to take the extra two minutes in the shower to get a good shave if I know I'm not the only one who is going to be experiencing the smoothness. So, when a guy exits your life, you can give yourself a little time to try being hirsute. Having toe hair might not be a turn-on, but it's an interesting conversation piece over brunch with the girls.

The nether region, however, is usually a hemisphere that's tended to for the sake of lovers and bikinis. So, unless you're planning a day at the beach, a breakup is a good time to take a little vacation from your waxing lady (she'll understand) and experience the joy of a springy, fluffy, full bush. Enjoy it while you can, because it's a little-known fact among young women, but when you're older, it'll start to go away on its own.

So get to know your pubes, girls, before it's too late.

Embrace Your Friends

My grandma used to say that the daytime was for your girlfriends and the evening was for your boyfriend. Well, nix the boyfriend and suddenly your evenings are free for girl time, too.

Boyfriends come and go (and sometimes the same one might come and go more than once), but friends usually have sturdier footing in our lives. And the time in between relationships is the best time to enjoy the girls (or guys) you cherish most as friends. Cry on their shoulders if you need to, and when your tears dry, fall back in love with your friends—it's a love that can be a lot simpler than the love you felt for your ex. And it doesn't require a depilatory.

Look Really Awful While You're Sleeping

Somehow, sleeping in a bed with someone else has become a necessary part of a relationship. Being single, however, lets us ladies return to our natural state of slumber. That's right: sleeping solo means you can sprawl out in the middle of the bed with as many or as few covers you please. Feel free to wear your favorite flannel nightgown—the one with teddy bears on it—or that cozy old *90210* T-shirt with holes in it. Get out the tattered stuffed animal (Binky!) you were embarrassed to sleep with when your ex was around. Then make sure you've taken care of all the other sleep musts: Have you inserted your retainer and slapped on the teeth-whitening strips? Did you put on the spider vein–reducing support hose? Have you applied an opaque pimple cream and that sour-smelling lotion that reduces the look of fine lines around your eyes? While you're at it, throw some rollers in your hair, put in earplugs, and take out your false teeth. Now you are ready to curl up, close your eyes, and pass gas.

Be Unabashedly Selfish

Breaking up with a guy can be a little bit like quitting a part-time job. Women are often the givers in a relationship. We're usually the rememberers of birthdays, the buyers of groceries, and the strokers of egos. These tasks can seem second nature when you're in a relationship—they can even be fun and comforting—but relieving yourself of

PROFILES IN NOT-A-LOT-OF-COURAGE

Vira Hladun-Goldmann

In 1998, a sixty-three-year-old New Yorker, Vira Hladun-Goldmann, received the largest court-settled equitable divorce in U.S. history, walking away with 50 percent of the $86 million fortune she had shared with her former husband, Robert Goldman, sixty-five, chief executive of the Congress Financial Corporation.

For a wife to receive such a large percentage in that income bracket was unprecedented, but Hladun-Goldmann—who hyphenated her maiden name and inexplicably added an extra *n* to *Goldman* following the split in order to separate herself from her ex—made a convincing case that her role as Goldman's wife had been a major factor in his amassing his great wealth.

Goldman died two months after the divorce came through.

Had she not divorced him, she would have inherited 100 percent of his wealth.

But this divorce doyenne says she has no regrets. "Divorce is a stage of life, if you need it to be. It gives you an opportunity to start new and clean and get rid of the old!" she said. "Wherever Robert is, he's looking down on me and he's glad I'm happy."

these duties can be amazingly liberating. It can free up time and even money. So what are you going to do with this newfound autonomy? Whatever you'd like! Flirt. Write in your diary. Learn Spanish. Get a weekly deep-tissue massage. Play Joni Mitchell songs on the guitar. Hire a cleaning person. Join a fancy gym. Ignore everyone else's birthday and plan a big party for yourself instead. Plant sunflowers. Go to Aruba with your best friend. Stay in bed all day reading magazines. Get a puppy. Nap. Buy a vibrator. Take a road trip. Go shopping. Bake cookies and eat the dough.

But be careful—you might have such a good time that you decide to postpone ever getting into a relationship again.

Breakup Trees

You've dated a lot of jerks.
But not every guy you're going to meet
from here on out is going to be a jerk.
Some of them will be assholes.

—ANNA JANE'S DAD

Behind every family tree is another tree of sorts—one that never took root. That would be the breakup tree, which charts all the limbs that splintered before you joined up with the branch that mattered most.

After a breakup, you're going to need something to keep you from drinking yourself into a puddle. So why not take the time to document your failed romances in the format we've provided? You'll discover some patterns, and in the end you'll have a pretty diagram to hang up next to your actual family tree. Try placing it prominently in your parents' den. They'll be so proud.

To get you rolling, we've sketched out the highlights of our own sad, sad trees. (We've changed our exes' names to prevent litigation.)

BREAKUP TREE FOR
ANNA JANE GROSSMAN, B. 1980

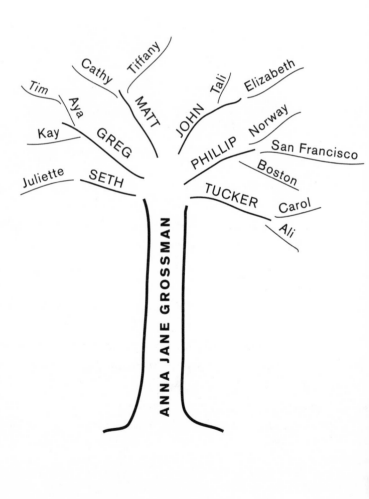

—**SETH,** b. 1980. Dated 4/92–5/92. Seth asked me out when we were in seventh grade. We went to the movies once or twice together with other kids, and those were our "dates." I kept waiting for him to kiss me, but he never did. He then broke up with me and told everyone—including the school nurse—that I was a prude.

—*Juliette,* b. 1981. The next year, Seth dated a girl at our school who had been in an after school–special TV movie with Oprah. She was nominated for an Academy Award a few years later, around the same time I was busy battling acne and depression.

—**GREG,** b. 1975. Dated 8/98–8/99. He was an artist and an athlete and was definitely my first love. He told me many times that our relationship wouldn't last because I didn't have as much relationship and breakup experience as he did, and therefore things weren't equal. I'm still not sure what this means. Even when we were getting along perfectly, he'd say things like, "You'll understand all of this better after we break up." Nevertheless, I adored him. On a road trip he took with a friend, he reunited with a girl named Kay he'd known in high school. I was told by a mutual friend she had a flat chest and mousy hair. When he returned, he broke up with me right after I'd taken a three-hour train ride to go to his friend's wedding with him. I took the next train home after he told me, and then pretty much cried for six months straight.

—*Aya,* b. 1971 Before he dated me, Greg dated a woman who was a bit older than him, named Aya. She was a chef who looked like Audrey Hepburn, which annoyed me.

—*Tim,* b. 1973 Aya later dated a good friend of mine, Tim. He stopped returning my calls when they started dating.

—*Kay*, b. 1975. After he dated me, Greg started dating Kay, the girl he'd reunited with. They built a house together and as far as I know continue to live happily stinking ever after. When he and I went out for a platonic drink a few years after we broke up, he accidentally referred to me by her name.

—**MATT,** b. 1979. Dated 4/00–12/01. I met Matt, a teacher who really liked doing African dance, in a writing class in college. We were friendly for a few months, and one day it suddenly dawned on me that he had a crush on me. I realized I liked him too. I kissed him first, and he often reminded me of this. He also said that if we ever got married, he hoped I'd propose to him. He was extremely sweet, and I often regret breaking up with him, but after a while I started to find him cheap and a bit arrogant, and this bugged me. Mostly, though, I think the whole relationship felt a little too serious for me at the time. When I broke up with him, he told me I didn't know how to be happy.

    —*Cathy*, b. 1979. Matt dated Cathy before he dated me. She later was our college's valedictorian. I don't know why they broke up. I think she was his first girlfriend.

    —*Tiffany*, b. 1980. Soon after we broke up, he met Tiffany at a wedding. I tried to get back together with him a few months after we split, but he was already passionately in love with her. It was a turn of events that was hard for me to swallow, even though I was the one to initially end things.

—**JOHN,** b. 1975. Dated 4/02–7/02. We also met in a writing class, but this was after I graduated. He had a beard and was into yoga and kabbalah. Truth be told, he bugged the hell out of me, but the sex was good and he got so upset every time I tried to break up with him that I decided it was easier to just stay together. He was a big crier. I finally gave him the boot on a whim when we were in an airport on our way to California to see his family. It suddenly hit me that this was not a man whose family I wanted to meet. So, I left the airport and went home while he flew to San Francisco in a rage, and then called me while drunk several times the following week.

—*Tali*, b. 1974. He met her in Israel and always told me that she looked just like Pocahontas. They dated the year before I met him. He said she complained that he didn't buy her enough gifts.

—*Elizabeth*, b. 1971. Immediately after he dated me, he dated another woman from our writing class. I know this only because he made an effort to tell me every detail about having sex with her when he'd call me drunk.

—**PHILLIP,** b. 1971. Dated 10/02–5/04. Phillip, a doctor and a scientist, picked me up at a party I was writing about for a newspaper. The whole time we dated, he was going back and forth from New York to Europe every few months to deal with family over there, and his constant coming and going created a lot of romance and a lot of stress in the relationship. But every time he'd go away, I'd get little packages delivered with no return address. One time there were Pop Rocks. Another time, a vintage edition of *Le Petit Prince*. He'd return with all kinds of clothing he'd bought secondhand for me in Europe. In the winter, we got drunk in a bus on our way to Atlantic City where we ran the table at craps. In the summer, we got soaked in the rain on Coney Island. At times, it all felt like something out of a movie. But then he moved to Boston for work, and he broke up with me; he wouldn't tell me why he so desperately wanted to break up, but I think it had to do with him wanting to try sleeping with Bostonites. What made it particularly difficult and confusing were his protestations (via e-mail) for many, many months after the breakup that he was still madly in love with me, but just wasn't capable of being in a relationship with me.

—*Norway,* b. 1969. I didn't know her name for most of the time we dated, because he always referred to her as Norway, which is where she was from. He didn't want to interject the baggage of past romances into our relationship, so he never used her real name, and in fact didn't talk about her a lot. They dated on and off for a decade and had a daughter.

—*San Francisco,* b. 1977. She was a dancer who lived in New York but broke up with Phillip shortly before I met him when she moved back to San Francisco. I didn't know much about her, except that she had a big butt and a collection of Britney Spears CDs.

—*Boston,* b. unknown. I know nothing about her except that she dated Phillip for several months after he moved to Boston. When she broke up with him, he came to see me in New York and told me once again that he was still madly in love with me . . . but wasn't capable of being in a relationship with me.

—**TUCKER,** b. 1976. Dated 11/04–3/05. Tucker was a teacher (like Matt) and a dancer (like Matt) and a scientist (like Phillip) who looked a little like Greg. We met at a Halloween party. I was dressed as Bettie Page. "You're the cutest girl here," he said. "And I'm the best-looking guy. We should get together." Idiot that I am, I said, "Okay," even though I had a suspicion he was gay. It was mostly the fact that he had a teacup-sized dog whom he let sleep in his bed. We became very serious pretty quickly, and then I think we quickly mutually lost interest in each other. After a while he was so uninterested in me that I started to suspect he was seeing someone else. Either that, or he was a closeted homosexual. After we broke up, my friends told me they'd all come to the latter conclusion the first time they met him. I'm still not sure.

—*Carol,* b. 1970. They dated when he was twelve and she was eighteen. I have no clue why an eighteen-year-old girl would want to date a twelve year old. The mental age difference is like two decades. He lost his virginity to her, which I think counts as statutory rape. She also convinced him to get a really bizarre-looking tattoo on his arm of an eyeball.

—*Ali,* b. 1976. Tucker and Ali dated for six years, but then he broke up with her. I don't really know what caused the breakup, but he was upset because she took all their mutual friends with her. He, however, got to keep the cookbooks and was very pleased about that.

BREAKUP TREE FOR
FLINT JASON WAINESS, B. 1974

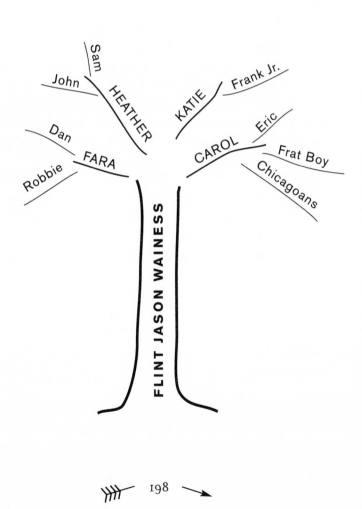

—**FARA,** b. 1973. Dated 6/90–8/90. She was five feet tall, and she had the most delicate voice. She was a walking set of oddities, a Jewish girl born on a farm in Missouri, raised barefoot but with a taste for fancy shoes. She was musically gifted, an aspiring opera singer. We met on a summer program called High School in Israel. We were fifteen but could do whatever we wanted, and what we wanted was to drink Macabee beer, listen to Pink Floyd, and tickle each other's naked bodies until my roommates got annoyed. After the summer, we wrote letters furiously. But when I finally went to visit her in Florida, I got mono and slept through the entire week. We slowly lost touch after that.

   —*Robbie,* b. 1972. Fara dated Robbie for the first half of the summer in Israel, but it was clear that they were just going through the motions. Fara and I would stare at each other across the folding tables at Shlomo's Kitchen. One night, on a beach in Netanya, Robbie was absent, and I replaced him by charming the pants off Fara, literally.

   —*Dan,* b. 1968. It's hard to track down Fara's history, so Dan is a composite. All I know is that Fara went on to date (and become) a born-again Christian and was in danger of becoming a Jew for Jesus. She also dated a military man, who may or may not have been the same guy. Somewhere out there, Fara is married with children. It may or may not be to Dan.

—**HEATHER,** b. 1977. Dated 1992–1993. I was a freshman in college; she was a junior in high school. She had the soul of a poet but the attitude of Lil' Kim. She had to sneak out of the house to see me, which made our trysts feel romantic as hell. She drove a tiny yellow car, and she drove it badly. When I was in the passenger seat of that car, I resolved to break up with her. But when I was out of the car and we were smoking chronic and listening to Thelonious Monk, I felt a happiness I am not sure I have ever matched. We made each other laugh so hard I had an asthma attack. But while I was cruising through college, Heather was failing out of high school, developing a drinking problem, and making her parents consider suicide. Although we were never officially together, we broke up at least thirteen times before it really ended.

—*John,* b. 1977. John was a proud Chaldean (Iraqi Catholic) who drove a Trans Am and had lots of gold chains. I'm pretty sure they were high school sweethearts while I was dating Heather. This may or may not have been related to the fact that I was jumped at a party and punched in the face repeatedly by seven Chaldean boys who said I had been with one of their girlfriends.

—*Sam,* b. 1975. This is Heather's husband. I believe he's a dry cleaner and supposedly very nice. I wonder if he knows her wild history. I wonder if he would care.

—**KATIE,** b. 1975. Dated 1994–1997. She was and will forever be my first love. It was college, so we had nothing to do except love each other. She wore sweatpants a lot. For three years, we were inseparable. She convinced me to eat sushi, and taught me the meaning of a "disco nap" and the value of patience when a Jewish girl blow-dries her hair. We broke up for a while, and so she decided to go to France for a semester. We got back together right before she left, and I promised that no matter what happened when she was gone, I wouldn't tell her while she was away. But when I went to visit her, I broke that promise, and left her sobbing in a London hotel room. I didn't know anyone had that many tears.

—*Frank Jr.*, b. 1975. Frank owns a chain of ice cream and candy shops. How could I ever have competed with that? Somehow, Katie has managed to lose ten pounds while dating him. They now live together and likely will marry, but Katie continues to have her doubts. Getting over me is tougher than you would think.

—**CAROL,** b. 1978. Dated 2000–2004. Carol and I still have an outside shot at working out, so I have to be careful here. We met through a mutual friend whom we later came to despise. She has big hair and the most beautiful eyes, but the most important thing to know about Carol is that she has the life force of a thousand villages. She feels, thinks about, and experiences life more forcibly than anyone I have ever known (too forcibly for me, sometimes). Her three hearts are all filled with nothing but love. We broke up because she went to law school in Chicago, and because I am a poor, slovenly screenwriter with a baseball fetish. We still talk regularly.

—*Eric,* b. 1975. This was Carol's first love. He was in college; she was in high school. Her family disapproved of him because he was older and not Methodist. His family didn't care enough about her to disapprove. They were Korean royalty, and it simply wasn't an option for him to select lily-white Carol. Eventually, Carol came to recognize a cruelty in Eric that allowed her to get over him.

—*Frat Boy,* b. 1977. Frat Boy and Carol dated in college. She thought it was casual; he thought it was serious. After they broke up, he kept professing his love loudly in college bars.

—*Chicagoans,* b. various. Since moving to Chicago, Carol has dated many, many men. But she has found that they all kind of blur together, all have the same interests, the same comments, the same lack of desire to live life fully.

Get Over It Survey Results

I've always been able to do this,
break up with someone and never look back.
Being alone: there's a certain dignity to it.
—JANET LIVERMORE, *SINGLES*

Our final survey results address how most mortals get over breakups—as if they have any clue.

In the weeks after a difficult breakup, roughly how much time each day do you spend thinking about your ex?

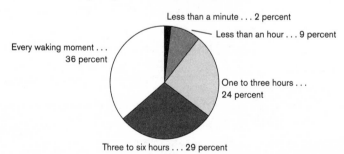

Less than a minute . . . 2 percent

Less than an hour . . . 9 percent

Every waking moment . . . 36 percent

One to three hours . . . 24 percent

Three to six hours . . . 29 percent

(That's right. Two-thirds of us spend between three hours and every waking moment every day thinking about that bad breakup. Think of the lost productivity!)

Get Over It

It usually takes me ___ to get over a bad breakup.

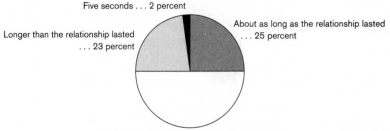

Five seconds . . . 2 percent

Longer than the relationship lasted . . . 23 percent

About as long as the relationship lasted . . . 25 percent

Less time than the relationship lasted . . . 50 percent

(Who are these 2 percent and why aren't they writing a book?)

I find myself doing the following more often than usual after a breakup:

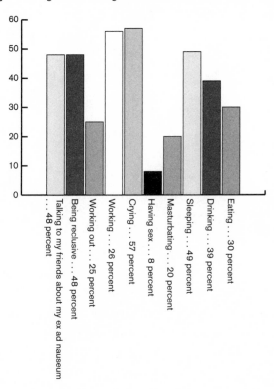

Talking to my friends about my ex ad nauseum . . . 48 percent

Being reclusive . . . 48 percent

Working out . . . 25 percent

Working . . . 26 percent

Crying . . . 57 percent

Having sex . . . 8 percent

Masturbating . . . 20 percent

Sleeping . . . 49 percent

Drinking . . . 39 percent

Eating . . . 30 percent

True or false: I've slept with an ex.

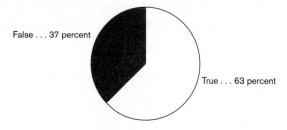

False . . . 37 percent

True . . . 63 percent

After a breakup, what do you usually miss the most?

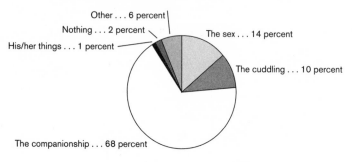

Other . . . 6 percent

Nothing . . . 2 percent

His/her things . . . 1 percent

The sex . . . 14 percent

The cuddling . . . 10 percent

The companionship . . . 68 percent

From the Trenches:
What's the Best Thing about
Being Single Again?

I love to shop after a bad relationship.
I buy a new outfit and it makes me feel better. It just does.
Sometimes if I see a really great outfit,
I'll break up with someone on purpose.

—RITA RUDNER

So you've read our essays extolling the glories of the unattached life. But our survey respondents had some thoughts of their own—some wise, some completely asinine—as to the best thing about being single again.

"The extra free time, same with the extra bed space." Kathryn, 23

"Going out any time I want. Meeting new people all the time. No more fighting and drama." Claire, 22

"All the women in NYC!" Justin, 19

"Can pass gas freely." Louise, extremely old

"Not having to second-guess yourself all the time because you're dating a jackass." Ellen, 24

"Banging everyone else." Allie, 23

"It's a new start." Joanne, 40

"Not having to wait for him to call so I can make plans." Debbie, 19

"Remembering the goals you had before you ever met the ex. Knowing that life can be happy and pleasant and hopeful without being in a relationship." Stephanie, 24

"Not having someone I feel I have to check in with, worry about, or feel guilty about." Peter, 20

"Eh, not much." Kal, 28

>>>>— **The Breakup-Party Primer** ——→

by Christine Gallagher

The end of a significant relationship is a major life event for most people. After the dust has settled and the haggling over possessions is done, this can be a great time to have a breakup party, to announce to the world that you're single and ready to mingle again.

Some people throw their own breakup parties. In other cases, the parties are organized by friends as a gesture of support to a pal who has been through Relationship Hell. A great party can bring much-needed fun and laughter to a difficult rite of passage.

So here's how to plan one.

1) Decide on the type of party you want to throw. Is it a wild, hilarious night with friends, or a more dignified event marking an important life transition? Unlike your wedding, this party isn't for your parents or family; this is for you.

"It sucks." Norma, 31

"Freedom!" Aeden, 28

"Looking forward to those new relationship butterflies." Leila, 34

"Not having to shave my legs." Kay, 30

2) Choose your guests carefully, weeding out anyone who won't "get it." Make suggestions for gifts people can bring, including everything that has been taken by the newly departed.

3) Book entertainment. Don't be bashful. If you want a stripper cop, book a stripper cop.

4) Provide breakup-party props. A dartboard with a picture of your ex is never a bad choice. And make sure to have a fire handy, to burn anything he left behind (you can auction off the more valuable possessions).

5) Plan a fun breakup-party menu in keeping with the party theme. A favorite is split pea soup followed by delicious banana splits. Don't be afraid to be corny.

6) And don't forget to have a slew of good breakup songs. For suggestions, see Flint and Anna Jane's favorite breakup songs (see page 222).

Christine Gallagher is the author of *How to Throw a Breakup or Divorce Party*. It's available at RevengeLady.com

"My cats and I have the bed to ourselves." *Sharon, 30*

"My ongoing love affair with two men, Ben and Jerry, can once again come out into the open." *Cait, 24*

"Porn at any time." *Tim, 24*

"The dating-debacle anecdotes." Daisy, 25

"Not having to check in with anyone besides my mother." Esther, 34

"Not putting up with the annoying crap that made you break up with them." Nina, 36

"I don't feel like I have to walk on eggshells anymore." Ashley, 20

"Furries, rabbits, and other toys." Katrina, 27

"My hand doesn't make me wear a condom." Monkey, 28

"I can watch all the NASCAR I want." Jade, 38

"No more action-figure collectibles in my apartment." Katie, 25

"Not having to remember to take birth control." CeCe, 33

"The toilet seat stays down." Marie, 30

"Being able to walk around naked in the morning without fear of getting ravished and having to hop back in the shower so you don't smell like sex at work." Almond, 29

Everything Else You Ever Wanted to Know about Getting Over It (but Were Afraid to Ask Dr. Phil)

More questions? We know, it's getting ridiculous. Can't you people break up for yourselves? But, the reality is, you keep asking us. And this is probably the trickiest section of all, because it's one thing to bungle the actual breakup but quite another to bungle the rest of your life after the breakup.

So we're going to try to answer these simply and succinctly, and then we're going to curl up in front of the television with three cakes, two cats, and one *Beaches* DVD, and this time we're going to yell at the TV until Hillary doesn't die.

Can I have sex with my ex after the breakup?

FLINT: Yes. But only if neither party wants to get back together and you're both drunk.

ANNA JANE: Most of us have done it, but it's still generally a bad idea. One of you will doubtless find the encounter more meaningful than the other. I suggest buying gold foil stars and putting one on your calendar for every day you go without contacting your ex. It will give you a sense of accomplishment—and it'll make your calendar so darn pretty!

Can I have sex with you after the breakup?

FLINT: Yes, but only if you are five-foot-seven, have blue eyes, straight dark hair, breasts larger than oranges but smaller than pineapples, have read the collected works of Charles Dickens, and love Leonard Cohen.

ANNA JANE: Flint, I'm not sleeping with you.

Can I have sex with my ex's friends and my friends' exes?

FLINT: Absolutely. This is highly encouraged, because most of the people we meet are through our friends and lovers. In other words, if we can't date our ex's friends or our friends' exes, we are destined to a life of loneliness and Internet dating. I firmly reject the popular philosophy "bros before hos," which posits that your feelings toward your friends always take precedence over your feelings toward a potential love interest. Don't be cruel about it by sleeping with a woman you don't really like whom your friend still loves. But if you and she have a real shot, do it.

ANNA JANE: I do know several people who have gone on to marry friends of their exes.

But if you date your friend's ex, you're probably going to soon be short one friend. Imagine it in reverse. Most of us like to imagine that our ex will never find happiness without us. We know this probably isn't going to happen, but it's not an awful thing to imagine. However, if your ex finds love in the form of one of your good friends, there's no way to keep the fantasy alive. Do you want to rip the security blanket of ignorance from your friend? Would that make you much of a friend? However, sleeping with your ex's exes should be avoided.

FLINT: Why?

ANNA JANE: Well, if you're dating your ex's ex—and I think this would mean that at least one of you has to be bisexual— you have to face the fact that you're probably trying to hurt your ex or your new lover is trying to hurt your ex, who would also be his or her ex. Basically, this is a situation that just involves way too many possessive pronouns.

FLINT: Okay, I get it if your ex dumped you. But if you were the one who did the dumping, if you *chose* not to date that person, don't you want your ex to find happiness? Even if it is with your friend? Don't be selfish. Stop being so selfish. (Also, do you want to make out?)

ANNA JANE: Yes, but not with you.

Will I ever love again?

ANNA JANE: Probably.

FLINT: Not.

ANNA JANE: Eventually. Of course, you might be shriveled when it happens. Or you might find the person you love doesn't love you. But, yes, you will probably love again at some point.

THE WEDDING BASHER:
TIPS FOR SURVIVING OTHER PEOPLE'S WEDDINGS

They're supposed to be a celebration of true love, two soul mates coming together with friends and family in order to show off their rented clothing.

Yet for many of us, weddings aren't such joyous occasions. The guest list typically runs around two hundred people. The bride and groom have a close relationship with approximately twelve of these people. Often, the guests have to fly in from far-away places. And what do they get for their trip? Overpriced plane fares, hotel bills, and, oh yeah, you still have to buy the couple a present that they have been so kind as to pick out for themselves through a registry.

It can often feel like the only people that truly enjoy these events are the parents of the bride and groom, and their enjoyment will most likely cease the next day when they check their bank accounts. While everything else in the world is constantly being reformed and reinvented, the modern wedding remains, for a lot of us, a dreary affair. Especially if you've recently been through a breakup.

But, don't despair, hope is on the way: here are four simple tips for surviving other people's weddings.

1) Don't touch the main course. You probably filled up on the hors d'oeuvres anyway. Why not just eat and eat? Because the only thing worse than waking up alone is waking up alone with the feeling that you're a big, fat marshmallow. So, if you have to skip something for the sake of your waistline, this is it.

   We won't go so far as to suggest brown-bagging the entrée; instead, we recommend skipping the chewy, tasteless main course and going straight for the dessert, and the dessert wine. Is there leftover cake? That's one food group where we do suggest the doggie-bag route. You'll be happy to have it for breakfast when you wake up hungover in a ditch.

2) Drink to excess. Obviously, if you're driving or sober or in AA, this one does not apply to you. But, if you're not, weddings are a perfect opportunity to get soused. This allows you to hit on people you wouldn't ordinarily hit on, and not roll your eyes when you tell the bride, "He's perfect for you." Ideally, it will lead to a late-night skinny-dipping session in the hotel pool. Maybe you'll even convince someone to join you.

3) Bring a really hot date even if you weren't invited to bring a date. This may sound completely inappropriate, but so is an invitation that makes you feel like a complete loser by assuming that you're so uncool you couldn't find a date even if you wanted to. So, bring a date, and he or she will find a place to sit. You're not eating the entrée anyway, so it's not costing the bride and groom extra. At the end of the night, you can either hook up with the hot date, or use the hot date as a wingman/wingwoman.

4) Dance, white boy, dance. It doesn't matter if you move like a three-toed sloth on PCP. Move that body around the dance floor. Dance with the old, the young, the huddled masses yearning to breathe free. Worst-case scenario, you sweat off a few pounds. Best-case, you ruin a wedding when you accidentally elbow the bride during the chicken dance.

FLINT: Not.

What's the line between healthy inquiry and stalking?

ANNA JANE: I think it has more to do with how you feel about what you're doing. If your ex were inquiring about you in the same way, would you be flattered? Hurt? Disturbed? Turned on? (Yay! He's finally taking an interest in me!) However, if you feel you can't trust your judgment, a restraining order is usually a sign that it's time to back off.

FLINT: "Healthy inquiry" includes calling and hanging up, plying your friends with truth serum and then asking questions about your ex's new relationship, and driving by your ex's house repeatedly while blasting Air Supply. It becomes stalking *when your ex knows* that you're driving by while blasting Air Supply and you continue to do so anyway.

Can I be friends with my ex?

FLINT: Yes. Absolutely. But only if you're BOTH in happy new relationships, or both single, or live in different cities. It's also critical never to reveal information about your current love life to your former flame. Even if you're friends, you're friends who have seen each other naked, and jealousy will always be an issue.

ANNA JANE: I've heard being friends with your ex is possible and can even be rewarding. But have I ever been able to do it? No. I once suggested to an ex that we could be friends if he became a monk. "I'd do it," he said, "but I'm Jewish."

If an ex who broke your heart comes back begging for a second chance, what should you do?

FLINT: Take her back, but only if the tables have truly turned. Every relationship has a boss, and you need to make sure that this time it's you.

ANNA JANE: I have to second Flint on this one, although I've often heard it's not a good idea to go backward. But if you feel like you can make it work this time, go for it. The second breakup can't be as bad as the first . . . right?

What's the worst thing about being single?

FLINT: You spend too much time thinking about girls. Wait, that's the worst part about being in a relationship, too. Drat!

ANNA JANE: In general, I think it's just not having the person around anymore—their love, their company, their friendship, and so on. But in my last relationship, the thing that was worst about being single was no longer being able to cuddle with my ex's dog. I really loved that crazy mutt.

How long before you should "get back on the horse"?

FLINT: Seven days. This may be the most important question in the wake of a relationship, and so, if my answer sounds glib, it isn't. The fact is, you need to get back out there immediately, not because you're going to meet someone right away (if you have a soul, it will take you a long, long time to recover from a failed relationship), but because it's important not to be alone at times like these, and it's important to put the long recovery process in motion. However, before starting the drinking and making out with strangers, you should take one week to let yourself feel the pain of losing the one you once loved. Lock yourself in your room, smoke cigarettes, drink bourbon, listen to the Smiths, eat frosted cupcakes, and just let yourself go.

ANNA JANE: Take as long as you need to heal and get over it. Sometimes in between relationships, you can reach a real calm. It's an empowering feeling, which reminds you that you don't need someone else in your bed in order to enjoy life. If you're craving a rebound, then go for it. But keep in mind that throwing yourself at the first thing that comes along may just result in having to go through another breakup a lot sooner than you would've liked.

)))—— **My Worst Breakup** ——→

by Wendy Kaufman

The first cut is the deepest, and this was a laceration of the highest order. Bruce was my first real love, you know, the first one who actually loves you back! Anyway, he was my college sweetheart and the guy I was going to run off into the sunset with. All signs were pointing to man-and-wifedom when he had to leave school a little earlier than expected due to his dubious association with a book of matches and the dorm elevator on a drunken Friday night. But, a little expulsion was not going to keep us apart; we had plans and dreams we discussed by phone every day.

With three hundred miles between us, and me being a realist, we agreed to see others, but to remain sexually faithful. Did I mention that I was young and naive at the time? Then, out of nowhere, I didn't hear from Bruce. I left some messages and sent a few letters, but no response. I was in a bit of a panic when I finally reached his mom. "Bruce is not available," she said like an efficient reception-ist, not at all sounding like the woman I had known for the past four years. She continued, "Didn't Bruce tell you? He got married." Insert knife, and twist . . . and twist. Can you think of anything WORSE than hearing that your boyfriend of four years just up and got married without telling you?

I was sick, felt faint, couldn't think, communicate, eat, or function. I was distraught for days. When I finally pulled myself together after hours of therapeutic conversations

(continues)

)))— 217 ——→

with family and friends, I received a ten-page letter telling me how sorry he was, how he still loved me, but that he had gotten someone pregnant and decided that he had to "do the right thing," which apparently did not include having the decency to let me in on his Marriage Plan B. I vowed that I would never be hurt like this again, never expose myself ever again to such pain.

Well, Bruce stayed in touch through the years while he was married, but for me, there were other boyfriends who came and went. When he eventually separated from his wife, he did show up again, about twelve years later. We started to see each other again, gave it the old postcollege try, but it was a colossal failure. The hopes and dreams that you share as kids are no longer relevant in the adult world, and he was stuck and angry at all the unresolved mistakes that he had made. At least this time around it was a mutual parting of the ways, which was far better than my Plan B, which was to have my mom call him and tell him to get lost.

> Wendy Kaufman is . . . finally happily married. At the young age of forty-six, her father gave her away, remarking to all the guests invited to her wedding that "All sales are final." She is also known as "The Snapple Lady."

Epilogue

P.S.: A Final Note
from Flint and Anna Jane

Dear John and Jane,

We hope you liked our book.

At this point, we expect you've mourned, moped, and Web stalked. You've also drunk dialed, antiqued, eaten entire cakes in one sitting, adopted cats, had long-winded conversations with those cats, illegally downloaded every song ever sung by The Smiths, gained weight, lost weight, joined an Internet dating service, angry dated, sucked the fumes out of a whipped cream bottle, and, of course, obsessed endlessly about how great it would be to get back together with us.

Now take a deep breath. It's time, once and for all, to break up with your breakup.

We know you're still thinking about us way more than you'll admit. We know you're certain you'll never find happiness again. We know you've become cynical and jaded and addicted to Internet porn.

But, the fact is, the whining needs to stop. Everyone is sick of it. For a while it was cute, but there is a statute of limitations on adorableness and you have passed it. You've gone from neurotic to clinical, and the only option you have at this point is to let go.

We know this might not be altogether possible, but here's some key advice: pretend.

That's right—make believe you're okay. Your insides are still mush, but that doesn't mean you can't wash your face, pour some coffee, and hit the town.

Yes, it's all a lie, but so was our relationship. Try going through the motions of a nonwounded person for a few weeks; if you can convince others that you're okay, you might one day convince yourself too.

One thing to remember is that you're not in a great rush. People live longer now. People get married later now. What does this mean? It means people get divorced later, too.

And what does *that* mean? It means that most of us spend the majority of our days alone, and that's okay.

Amazingly, aloneness can be good news, since you can't experience a crushing breakup if you're not coupled.

What's more, when you're comfortable being alone, the pressure to couple can be lifted off your shoulders and dating actually can be fun.

If you are indeed on the dating circuit, chances are you'll couple again. Before your dating days are done, you're going to reject dozens of suitors and be rejected by dozens of suitors, and then one day you'll magically wake up next to someone new and you'll find you're not thinking about us anymore. We know it sounds impossible, but it's true.

Oh, and next time you fall for someone, try to choose more wisely than you did last time. Avoid the immature and the insincere, and don't settle just because you're tired of being lonely.

The time right before you enter into a relationship is the time when you can afford to be most choosy. Once you meet someone new, your judgment is going to get cloudy, so take your time. You don't have to wait for "the one" because there probably isn't one "one." But that doesn't mean you can't wait for someone who makes you happy, who is worth the trouble of dating, loving, and breaking up with. Because, when you're back at Rock Bottom, it's important to know that it was worth it.

In other words, when you do pick someone to do the funky chicken with, make sure it's someone who is going to be worth all the trouble that may ensue when things don't work out—the trouble of, say, writing a whole book.

That's it, sweets. We miss you . . . just not enough to get back together with you.

Adios.

Anna Jane and Flint

P.S.: Your cats are extremely annoying. Please take them back.

The Breakup Songbook

What came first, the music or the misery?
People worry about kids playing with guns, or watching violent videos,
that some sort of culture of violence will take them over.
Nobody worries about kids listening to thousands, literally thousands,
of songs about heartbreak, rejection, pain, misery, and loss.
Did I listen to pop music because I was miserable?
Or was I miserable because I listened to pop music?

—ROB GORDON, *HIGH FIDELITY*

If there's one thing that can bring you to a place of calm or to a place of tears after a breakup, it's a song.

For your downloading pleasure, here are our favorite and least favorite heartstring-plunking breakup songs.

KEY
The following letters denote the mood, style, and/or spirit of the song:

    A—Angry
    C—Cheesy
    E—Empowering
    H—Hopeful
    N—Nostalgic
    P—Pathetic
    S—Sad
    *—Our Personal Favorites

Achy Breaky Heart (Billy Ray Cyrus) C
Against All Odds (Phil Collins) AN*
Ain't No Sunshine (Bill Withers) PCS
All by Myself (Celine) PC

All Out of Love (Air Supply) NP*

Alone (Heart) SH

Alone Again, Naturally (Gilbert O'Sullivan) P*

Are You Lonesome Tonight? (Elvis Presley) N*

At This Moment (Billy and the Beaters) CN

The Autumn Leaves (Nat King Cole) N*

Babe, I'm Gonna Leave You (Led Zeppelin) H*

Boyfriend (Ashlee Simpson) C

Breaking Up Is Hard to Do (The Carpenters) CN

The Breakup Song (The All American Rejects) AE*

Caroline (Outkast) AP

Carrion (Fiona Apple) SE*

Crazy (Patsy Cline) SP*

Cryin' (Roy Orbison) N*

The Crying Game (Boy George) HS*

Cry Me a River (Ella Fitzgerald) A*

Desperado (The Eagles) SNP*

Divorce (Tammy Wynette) CP

The Divorce Song (Liz Phair) AP

Does He Love You? (Reba McEntire and Linda Davis) A

Don't Cry Out Loud (Peter Allen) PC

Don't Give Up on Us, Baby (David Soul) H

Don't Go (Yaz) PC

Don't Go Breaking My Heart (702) P

Don't Know What You've Got (Cinderella) N*

Don't Speak (No Doubt) AC

Don't Turn Around (Ace of Base) P

Drive (The Cars) A

End of the Road (Boyz II Men) C

Everybody Hurts (REM) SC

Everything Reminds Me of Her (Elliott Smith) S*

Every Time You Go Away (Hall & Oates) PN
Famous Blue Raincoat (Leonard Cohen) SN*
Fifty Ways to Leave Your Lover (Paul Simon) H*
Fire and Rain (James Taylor) PN*
First Cut Is the Deepest (Cat Stevens) S*
Fuck and Run (Liz Phair) AC
Girlfriend in a Coma (The Smiths) H
Girl from New York (Of Montreal) P*
Gonna Get Along without You Now (Patience and Prudence) E
Good-bye to You (Michelle Branch) C
Good Morning, Heartache (Billie Holiday) S*
The Grass Is Blue (Dolly Parton) SN*
The Hardest Thing (98 Degrees) C
Hard Habit to Break (Chicago) NH*
Have a Nice Rest of Your Life (Randy Travis) P
Heartbreak Hotel (Elvis Presley) C*
Heart of Glass (Blondie) H*
Here's a Quarter, Call Someone Who Cares (Travis Tritt) ACE
Hopelessly Devoted (Olivia Newton-John) P*
How Am I Supposed to Live without You (Michael Bolton) PC
How Can You Mend a Broken Heart? (Bee Gees) P*
How Do I Live? (LeAnn Rimes and Trisha Yearwood) P
How Do You Like Me Now?! (Toby Keith) A
How Long's a Tear Take to Dry? (Beautiful South) S*
I Can't Forget You (Gloria Estefan) NC
I Can't Make You Love Me (Bonnie Raitt) PN*
I'd Rather Be Blue over You (Barbra Streisand) CP
I'd Rather Be Sorry (Kris Kristofferson and Rita Coolidge) HS
I Fall to Pieces (Patsy Cline) DNA*
If You Leave Me Now (Chicago) DN*
I Hate Everything about You (Ugly Kid Joe) A

I Just Died in Your Arms Tonight (Cutting Crew) NCP

I'll Be Watching You (Sting) NS

I'm Gone (Dolly Parton) AC

I'm Not in Love (10cc) CS*

Iris (The Goo Goo Dolls) P

It Must Have Been Love (Roxette) CPH

It's Too Late (Carol King) AH

I Will Always Love You (Dolly Parton) CN

I Will Survive (Gloria Gaynor) HP

Just Another Lonely Day (Ben Harper) NH

Last Dance with Mary Jane (Tom Petty) N

Last Good-bye (Jeff Buckley) S*

The Last I Saw Richard (Joni Mitchell) N*

Let It Die (Feist) S*

Live without Your Love (Wind Jammer) C

Love Bites (Def Leppard) AH

Lovefool (The Cardigans) P

Love Hurts (Nazareth) S

Love on the Rocks (Neil Diamond) PNH

Lush Life (Nat King Cole) PS*

Lyin' Eyes (Eagles) NA

Makin Whoopie (Ray Charles) PN

Me and Bobby McGee (Janis Joplin) NCS*

Mr. Big Stuff (Aretha Franklin) E

Not Getting over You (Terri Clark) P

Nothing Compares 2 U (Sinead O'Connor) PS*

Nothing Is Good Enough (Aimee Mann) A

November Rain (Guns N Roses) NHA*

One (Three Dog Night) PS

Only the Lonely (Roy Orbison) NH*

Oops, I Did It Again (Britney Spears) CP

The Other Woman (Nina Simone) S
Piece of My Heart (Janis Joplin) AE*
Separate Lives (Phil Collins) NAH
Should've Known Better (Richard Marx) C*
Since U Been Gone (Kelly Clarkson) E*
Single (Everything But The Girl) N
So Long, Marianne (Leonard Cohen) SN
Somebody Kill Me (Adam Sandler) AS
Somebody That I Used to Know (Elliott Smith) SN*
Song for the Dumped (Ben Folds Five) ANH*
Stay (Lisa Loeb) N
Still Got the Blues (Gary Moore) N
Tainted Love (Soft Cell) C
Tears on My Pillow (Little Anthony & The Imperials) NCPS*
There's a Fine, Fine Line (Avenue Q) S
Time Is on My Side (The Rolling Stones) H
Total Eclipse of the Heart (Bonnie Tyler) CPAH*
Truck Driver Divorce (Frank Zappa) C
Tubthumper (Chumbawamba) H
Unbreak My Heart (Toni Braxton) CP
Under Pressure (David Bowie and Queen) S*
Walk Away, Renee (The Four Tops) NH
Walk on By (Cake) PN*
Walk on By (Dionne Warwick) E
The Way We Were (Barbra Streisand) NPC*
What Becomes of the Brokenhearted? (The Temptations) C
What's Love Got to Do with It? (Tina Turner) EA*
When Can I See You Again? (Babyface) P
Where Did Our Love Go? (Soft Cell) CN
White Flag (Dido) CN
Why? (Annie Lennox) S

Wicked Game (Chris Isaak) CAN*

With or without You (U2) NH*

You Can Have Him (Nina Simone) AES*

You Had Me (Joss Stone) A

You Oughta Know (Alanis Morissette) A

You've Lost That Lovin' Feeling (Hall & Oates) NS

The Burn Book

Most of us will have more exes in our lives than we'll care to remember, but forgetting them might only lead to repeating mistakes. Here, we offer a space to do a little journaling so that you can keep track of all the louses you've loved and loathed.

Name: _____

Date of birth: _____

Dates dated: _____

How we met: _____

How we broke up: _____

The song that makes me think of this ex most is: _____

Name: _____

Date of birth: _____

Dates dated: _____

How we met: _____

How we broke up: _____

The object I most regret leaving at this ex's house is: _____

Name: _____

Date of birth: _____

Dates dated: _____

How we met: _____

How we broke up: _____

The curse word that best describes this ex would be: _____

Name: _____

Date of birth: _____

Dates dated: _____

How we met: _____

How we broke up: _____

This ex has this many hits on Google: _____

Place Photo Here

Name: _____

Date of birth: _____

Dates dated: _____

How we met: _____

How we broke up: _____

The part of the body where I would most like to punch this person would

be his or her: _____

Place Photo Here

Epilogue

Name: _____

Date of birth: _____

Dates dated: _____

How we met: _____

How we broke up: _____

This ex owes me $ _____

Name: _____

Date of birth: _____

Dates dated: _____

How we met: _____

How we broke up: _____

The thing I miss most about this ex is: _____

Name: _____

Date of birth: _____

Dates dated: _____

How we met: _____

How we broke up: _____

This breakup put me in therapy for _____ years.

Name: _____

Date of birth: _____

Dates dated: _____

How we met: _____

How we broke up: _____

The STD that I hope this ex gets is: _____